FRANSCHHOEK MEMORIES

with best wishes

Gwen Jennings

FRANSCHHOEK
MEMORIES

Life in the French Valley

GWEN JENNINGS

DOUBLE
STOREY
a juta company

First published 2004 by Double Storey Books, a division
of Juta & Co. Ltd, Mercury Crescent, Wetton, Cape
Town, South Africa

ISBN 1-919930-79-5

Edited by Priscilla Hall
DTP by Claudine Willatt-Bate
Printed by Creda Communications, Epping, Cape Town

Contents

Preface

This book is a record of the past, the past of the author and the many people who have shared with her their own recollections. Franschhoek is, for some, now a moneyed and sophisticated neighbourhood. For others, it is as it has always been. There is no way to judge what others might say of what one has remembered.

Thomas Macaulay, a historian of great repute in a bygone age, likened history to a broad and strong river carrying everything along in its relentless flow. Here, forests, bridges and nations are being washed away. There, bodies from sieges, epidemics and earthquakes bob along with the debris of mighty civilisations. Like ships in that river were the pagans, Moors, British traders and others of every kind.

Sometimes the river was placid, and peace reigned on earth for a time. Then the river, flooded now, sped over the edge of a cataract. It brought prophets and plunderers, skills, seeds and songs, nationalities and new genes, to an unsuspecting people down river. While all these cataclysmic events were precipitated by the river itself, people living along the riverbanks stood awed, terrified or simply astonished by what they witnessed.

This book is about those people, amongst whom I count myself, in a valley in Africa, watching destinies and events unfold, with no defence except our acquiescence. They watch from the banks of the river, aware of their fragile existence, and they say, 'I was there,' but mostly they go on living out their own destinies. In this book I want to draw pictures of those lives, my own included. They are unheralded and unsung, but complete in themselves.

The stories from the Valley people are in their own words. They are eloquent words, slowly thought out, and not easily forgotten. I have kept my voice out of their narrations as much as possible. Their memories and fine eye for detail are impressive. Their lives have not all been easy, but those lives, ordinary and yet extraordinary, tell of simple pleasures, love of family, the landscape and the seasons of which they are so much a part.

Like any wanderers, from Odysseus to Huckleberry Finn, whose stories explain why they had their journeys and adventures, I find myself at the beginning, knowing it for the first time. I tell the story, not because I am in the story, but because the story is in me.

Acknowledgements

To my sons, who continually said, 'Ma, when are you going to write a book?' and the many close friends who have remained supportive of me through thick and thin.

To Gorry Bowes-Taylor and Fleur MacFarlane; they sent me to Bridget Impey and Russell Martin at Double Storey, who, from the first, could not have been more enthusiastic and positive about the project.

To my brilliant editor, Priscilla Hall, to whom I am grateful for shaping the text and using her critical eye and erudition to re-organise and make this book work.

To say 'thank you' to the many people in Franschhoek is very difficult; so many, during my farming days, gave me so much that I can never adequately express my appreciation. For telling me the intimacies, joys and pain of their lives, without reservation, thanks are inadequate. My gratitude to Mary and Peter May, Japie and Maria Daniels, Alice and Miesie, Rooi Jan, Niel and Laura le Roux, Krige and Christine Siebrits, Paulina Daniels, Linkie, Dene, Emily, Apolly (whose Grandpa raised him on the farm), and Dinie Daniels, for her amazing support and knowledge, which helped me through the first season of farming.

Thanks to La Bri and Siggie and Pam Michelson for their constant encouragement and good dinners; Paddy and Graham Howes, particularly for the photographs; John, Carol and Mark

Dendy-Young, for help then and now, in excess of anything I can thank you for; Ludwig Maskie at La Cotte, for the best French cheeses south of Paris; Shirley and Lennart Parkfelt for music and roses; Peter for relaying his story; Angela Brink for stories, lunches and company; Michael and Grace for much help in the farming days; Dawn and Tom Darlington, for advice and help and fine talk; my friends Annette, Lesley, Nigel, Michael, Hilary P, Hilary R, Annie WB, Tizzi, Stephano, Peter and Liz, Trevor and Anne for their enthusiasm, Colin and Dorothy for critical comment and hospitality, Leigh Thomson for wise words, Michael and Margaret Scott for their enduring love and support; Evi, for enthusiasm; cousin Sarie for botanical and family information and enduring love and support; my sister Yvonne, my real link to family; my ever-willing neighbours, Pat Jacoby for great help, Michele Jacoby, and Virgo Martin for fixing computer panics at all hours as graciously as you have done.

To the staff of the Franschhoek Museum, especially Anna-Marie Burger, who from first reading of the script was totally enthusiastic, and Una Malherbe, for information, hours of help and photographs which appear on pages 1, 15, 42, 63, 152 and 210. To the owners of the estate Allée Bleue, who most graciously gave permission for me to use their marvellous old photos on pages 33, 45, 74 and 184.

The cause of all of this was Bill H, who insisted we move to Franschhoek: without you, this book would not have been written.

And finally to Mavis and my Angels, for arranging all of this, at the right time, with the right people, and for making me realise each day that love is the most important force in my life, and the most empowering.

To my three beloved sons, Roland, Eric and Peter,
my sister Yvonne, and cousin Sarie,
with great love and appreciation for having come into my life,
and for you, my love.

In memory of Martin and Peetie, my 'constant gardeners'.

And to the many people of Franschhoek
who have shared their life stories with me.
Without them, this book could not have been written.

1

Arrival in Franschhoek

In December 1985 I went to stay with Archie and Annette in Cape Town, which was a welcome break from Johannesburg, where I lived. The companionship with true and enduring friends was a cure for a hectic working life, and the beauty of the mountains and the sea was balm to the spirit. My partner, Bill, came down to join me between Christmas and New Year, and my sister and father were also in Cape Town, staying with cousins.

My father, who had been orphaned at a young age, had later been sent to be a boarder at the Franschhoek school with two slightly older brothers. Now, many years later, he was longing to have another look at the village where he had found some order and security during the years 1918 to 1923.

As it was a lovely day with a high sky and cool breeze, the mountains as beautiful as the travel brochures said they would be, Bill and I elected to take him for a day's outing to Franschhoek. We booked lunch at a newly launched restaurant, which was spoken of as the pride of the wine-growing areas. It was called 'Le Quartier Français' and was owned by Arthur and Ardre McWilliam-Smith. Susan Huxter has developed it beautifully since then, but right from the start it was a fine place for a meal.

Ardre was welcoming and knowledgeable. Her starter, a complex salad of subtle flavours, was exquisitely presented. The dessert consisted of one of her individual plum tarts, in an almond base with buttery pastry, and was proof that she had learnt her lessons well at Chartres, in France. The meal was in a class all of its own.

It was a marvellous happy lunch, and in this state of bonhomie induced by gastronomic heaven, we went up to the school so that Daddy could reminisce about his youth. While we walked about the buildings, a member of the staff asked us if he could be of help. Daddy told him he was an 'old boy' and we were immediately invited to come into the office.

Many old photographs were shown. Generations of grave-faced children gazed back steady-eyed from the pictures. The class teachers were also of a different ilk. Sedately dressed prim ladies, benign but unsmiling, they were obviously in charge of their own destiny and the children in their care. These were teachers who would teach.

I looked at other photographs of the staff and parents. In the faces there was a subtlety of character and a variety of attitudes. There was fortitude, serenity and humour, also self-respect. One teacher looked a bit fierce; he might well be difficult in class, but these were the normal hazards of life. The male teachers wore proper suits for the photographs; it was a serious business, this taking of one's image for posterity. Suits, stiff collars, haircuts with partings arrow-straight, beards and moustaches trimmed and in a few cases pomaded. Erect posture and a dignified expression were mandatory. The headmaster wore a frock coat and an expression of indisputable authority.

One noticed that not all of the children had uniforms. The shirt and pants for the boys came in many variations. If one had the misfortune to be the younger son or daughter, and finances were precarious that year, then the older children's clothes were 'renovated' with surprising originality. Not all of the children wore shoes.

A photograph of my father appeared, and his very young face wore, then, a look of helplessness and confusion. He was a child lost in fear and uncertainty. Daddy looked at himself for a very long time in silence. I caught his eyes as he looked up, and saw that he was overwhelmed with tears to find his past so unexpectedly put before him. Any recollection of his traumatic childhood was too much for him. I suggested a walk around the village to recover himself and relocate in his mind what he remembered of it.

The houses and gardens presented, at first glance, a calm and ordered existence. There were vegetable gardens at the side of many of them, coops of chickens here and there, ducks and geese wandering freely. Farm-type vehicles stood around, some in a state of advanced dilapidation. I began to look much more closely.

Every decent village should have a church and a graveyard. Franschhoek had three churches and two graveyards. I wondered idly if three churches represented a more moral or pious population. In colour the population, pious or otherwise, occupied a spectrum from cream to light chocolate. There were many styles of architecture: modern Cape Dutch, Victorian cottages with sagging broekie-lace verandas, a few unsuccessful attempts at Cape Georgian, yellow face-brick, and the straight Cape cottage. There were some nicely proportioned windows, a few with cardboard patched across broken panes of glass. There was also an orange-painted house, and one with purple walls and blue doors and windows.

Botanical enthusiasm seemed to have run rampant, out of control. Design was nowhere – more was clearly considered better.

There were outbursts of colour, some as garish as firecrackers. In this high summer, plants fought to get their faces to the sun, stretched out their tendrils, took possession of each other's positions in the flowerbeds. A jumble of shrubs and flowers sometimes threatened access to front doors, and windows were obscured by vigorous vines.

Hydrangeas grew to five feet, the flower heads larger than dinner plates. There were dahlias in crayon colours, black pansies, blue and red delphiniums, an abandoned quince hedge bent with globes of fruit which were teeming with wasps. Marigolds were planted in shrieking oranges and yellows, and a bit of maroon cockscomb had sprouted up in between them. A philadelphus was having an entanglement with an unsuitable companion in the next bed. Tree-sized camellias stood with petticoats of dropped flowers around their feet.

Overlaying all the plants were roses. They climbed, looped, sprawled, stood to attention, flopped, dangled, poked their heads through inappropriate spaces – in one garden between sunflowers – romantically draped themselves around old water tanks, choking less hardy species, and clearly were the most used and loved flowers of Franschhoek. The colours ranged from virginal white to the deepest, most passionate reds. These were not docile roses. They looked as if they were spitting on their hands, to see where else they could gain a foothold, to blossom extravagantly for all the world to admire.

In one garden I recognised roses of French origin. A honeysuckle had got its tendrils up the skirt of Madame Isaac Pereire; as one knows, French women of sophistication permit these things. The rose Tuscany was sprawled over a shed roof and was seeking further handholds on a wisteria which seemed to be losing the battle. The drooping clusters of pale mauve flowers were threaded through with the wine-red blooms of the rose.

A great sprawl of colour up a narrow dirt road attracted my attention. We turned up the road to see what it was. But there was a tree to be investigated first, on the opposite side of the sandy lane. Beneath it sat a silent group of caramel-coloured women in a tableau of slack-limbed Oriental lassitude. Their eyes were half shut, giving their faces a look of having retreated elsewhere. One of them was breast-feeding a naked child who wore a look of profound infant bliss on his face as he sucked on his mother and gripped his little penis in a podgy hand. A huge dark-winged and lacy butterfly flapped lazily past through the torpid air. The unreal atmosphere of this scene was heightened by the cloying perfume coming from a tumbled hedge of jasmine in full flower.

The shade under the tree was so dense that no rays of sun filtered through it. The leaves, an intense dark green and almost fleshy to the touch, reminded me of my Indian aunt's description of some trees in India which resembled rubber trees, but had a huge triangular shape.

While I was trying to identify this species, a conversation started behind me. I turned around to look and listen. 'Now, Jamie, I have had enough. I have given you five wives, not just one, but five. Your conduct is disgraceful! Your wives are waiting at home, and you are still courting the ladies next door. Every day I have to come and fetch you. Your father is outraged, so come home at once!' The accent of this delivery was educated, upper-class colonial.

A rounded woman with white hair rolled into a bun, pinned into her neck with a tortoiseshell clip, had lifted the lower edges of her full-length apron in both hands and was trying to shoo a small golden-coloured duck back into her property. A sign at the entrance said 'Lavender Cottage' in flowing script, and printed formally beneath was the name B Hardres-Williams.

She wore a blue patterned frock, under which I could see the firming outlines of a corset, and blue felt slippers with multi-coloured pom-poms on the front. She had a modest string of pearls around her neck, and a slender chain which carried a small cross. She reminded me, with unexpected emotion, of my mother. Her determination and coercion had convinced Jamie to return to his harem. The gate closed after Jamie was captured, and he waddled up the path loudly calling out to his wives. It sounded like an avian version of 'Honeys, I'm home'.

Along the garden wall were more roses, but unlike any I had ever seen. I later learned that some of them were *Rosa rugosa*, and the pink ones were originally called Japanese roses. *Rosa rugosa* and multiflora crosses were used in America along roadways as a living crash barrier to catch cars that ran off the road. It appeared unlikely that cars would be doing excessive speeds up this dead-end sandy lane, but the dense and thorny wall of roses provided formidable burglarproofing.

The stems of the roses growing over this garden wall were thick, and there was hardly a centimetre without vicious thorns. Their owner did not believe in pruning. They towered overhead, and I calculated that some of them were over six metres long. The arching stems were thickly covered in clusters of blooms, some in unusual colours, and their shapes were everything from the flat-faced five-petalled ones to the most sublime quartered roses with ruffled flowers like carnations, only twice as big.

I could guess the nature of the owner of each garden by what they had created. Some painfully neat gardens represented the labours of an orderly mind for whom discipline was everything, both in the manner of living their lives and in the expression of their garden. Hedges must have been clipped with nail scissors. A dropped leaf would cause consternation. The few flowers that were permitted would probably smell of air-freshener.

Other gardeners were besotted with their plants, owned sixteen varieties of pelargoniums, had sleepless nights about the newest hybrid oxalis, and suffered anxiety attacks about possessing a new clematis. I am one of these, so I am sympathetic to visible addictions. Besides which, real gardeners – even if they are parish priests – have no morals. If they did, Kew Gardens in England would not exist, nor would tulips have conquered the world. Gardeners are all accomplished thieves; the practice they indulge in is called 'taking a slip'.

Cows were tethered on grass verges, and lay down in luscious kikuyu grass. A donkey cart passed us, loaded with children who all wore masks and were singing noisily. A turkey who had survived Christmas, his neck and one wing bare of feathers suggesting an energetic escape from being on the Christmas menu, was scratching in an untidy bed of ripening pumpkins. A small spotted dog, panting in the heat, was pulling his elderly owner at the other end of the lead for a walk round the block.

I looked at the road signage. Station Street had been tampered with. 'Station' had been painted out, and 'Siesstraat' informed one of the location of the siding. This act of sedition may have been in protest about a lingering and pungent odour we noticed. The habit of alfresco urination for men is entrenched in the countryside. After all, alchohol drunk in generous quantities leads naturally to an urgent desire for relief, with a certain disdain for etiquette. I found all of this quite normal, having grown up on a farm where in or out of doors was only an academic illusion, and answering a call of nature behind the nearest bush was a minor delay on the journey to new adventures.

We noticed a lot of 'For Sale' notices wherever we walked in the village. They made no impression on me as I was gainfully and happily running my own business in Johannesburg, and moving to the Cape had never crossed my mind. The days passed by with friends, trips to the beaches, and other socialising. Bill left to return to Johannesburg.

A day or two later I received a call from him. 'Gwen, I was just thinking, why don't you look at one of those houses in Franschhoek. I know they would be cheap. We could buy one for holidays.' I disabused him of the idea immediately. I had a thriving business in Johannesburg which took all my energy. If I wanted to travel, it would be to Europe.

Two days later he phoned again. He had found an agent who

was going to show me houses. I went viewing with that agent and one or two others. Before I left Cape Town, Bill flew down and approved a house and small farm. We were to come down at Easter to sign all the papers, and move to a new life in June 1986.

This new purchase, Little Farm, was up the Pass Road, with a spectacular view of the Valley. Its name was officially Patrysfontein (Guineafowl Fountain), and part of the land lay across the road and further up the mountainside. Its water supply was an ancient year-round spring which had flowed off the mountain 'forever'. It was shared by the municipality through a *deelkas*, a box with two water pipes leading to different places. Our immediate neighbours were the Dendy-Youngs, the hugely popular restaurateurs at La Petite Ferme.

Little Farm really was a small farm, but it was also a play on the farmer's name, which was Ben Klein. He had married Flo late in life, and they were enjoying the tranquil country life and each other's long-searched-for love. Ben was an enthusiast, educated and capable, and attracted to anything new and fascinating, so various new styles of this and that were tried out. He farmed baby beef, which was a first in the Cape. All the cows had numbers, and he would stand at the pens and say, 'No. 7, No. 15, No. 22, come here,' and they unfailingly did. He explained that he couldn't eat anything with a name, and he enjoyed baby beef.

After Ben had been on a trip to Israel, he came back and decided to use drip irrigation, which he had seen working in that semi-desert, on his grapevines and his fruit trees. This was greeted in the Valley with much laughter and suspicion. 'You are going to do *what?*' the old farmers said. Drip by drip, what a waste of time! And all those hoses lying there, doing nothing most of the time. Ja well no fine.

❖

My father and I drove down from Johannesburg. My mother had died six years before, and he was delighted to be having an adventure in a place he loved. My sister and I decided he should stay with me for the summer, and spend winter at home in Rivonia. Loving Franschhoek as he did with such a passion, he was tremblingly excited at the prospect of spending six months there with me every year. And Bill was coming down within the month; he said so himself. Well, he did come down four months later, for a visit.

It was as Voortrekkers that we left family and friends, and set off on the journey. The car was filled with last-minute things, we were seriously overloaded, so it was to be a leisurely two-day trip arriving on a Sunday. Stuttaford's were bringing my worldly goods down to be delivered on Monday.

Leaving friends and family had been difficult and tearful, because Johannesburg was the only home I had known. When I told friends and relatives we had bought a farm in Franschhoek, their reaction was one of disbelief. 'Tell us again, Gwen, where is this place? It must be at the end of the world, no one has ever heard of it, and who lives there anyway?'

To the Huguenots arriving in the 1680s, it really must have seemed to be at the end of the world, so I chose to explain. 'Well, you see, if you leave Cape Town and then head north-east on the N1 for fifteen kilometres, you will come to the top of a hill, and there before you is a valley. Look towards the right, and you see the prehistoric shape of the Simonsberg and the misty outline of the Drakenstein and Hex River mountains. Then you drive another fifteen kilometres and you pass Joostenberg, which was once the end of the world for many people, and Muldersvlei. And if you go further, you come to Paarl. Now Paarl had thought it was the end of the world, before the vast and lonely Karoo, but if you turn to your right and follow the Berg River, you are getting closer. Then the old people would say you were at the end of the world, but it is not so. There are still the farms of De Hoop, L'Arc d'Orléans, Plaisir de Merle, L'Ormarins, La Motte, La Provence, La Cotte, La Bourgogne, Champagne, La Colline, and La Dauphine. As you go further into this valley, you come to a small village, and that is Franschhoek.'

These city girls look nonplussed. 'Mmm,' they said. I explained that it was also close to both Paarl and Stellenbosch. To Johannesburg cognoscenti, anything beyond the 'grape curtain' of the Western Cape was foreign, the notable exceptions being Clifton beach, Kenilworth racetrack, Table Mountain, the Mount Nelson and Constantia. 'They speak Afrikaans all the time. How will you understand them?' Didn't we live in a bilingual country? 'It rains without stopping for the whole winter.' Don't you watch the weather reports? 'Furthermore, you can't have a live-in maid' – this last said with expressions of a major disaster overtaking one's life. It was unthinkable to move there willingly.

Further salvoes included: 'Where are you going to have lunch, without Stephanie's?' Stephanie's was the all-hours pit stop for all us speedsters living in Hyde Park and Sandhurst. Besides the amazing salads, the presence of the proprietors Werner and Stephanie was a magnet. Advice was given to the lovelorn, babies were patted and shown around the kitchen, a new hairstyle elicited fulsome compliments, and the coffee was the best in town. It was packed morning till night. I am pleased to report Stephanie's has now relocated to Somerset West, and is still as good as ever.

I explained that I planned to survive, and they might even be persuaded to come and visit. There was a noticeable lack of enthusiasm.

In spite of all these adverse comments, Daddy and I set off on a cold and rainy Highveld morning for our new home. Daddy had told me all the stories from the memories of his time at the hostel. The high-school boys were employed in a pack-shed during the fruit season to make wooden crates in which the fruit was carefully packed to go to market or to be exported. They were paid one shilling for a hundred crates, and beside them was a large box with fruit to eat. It was refilled continually.

After getting a lift to Cape Town for a weekend's courting, he recalled, he had missed the train coming home and walked back to Franschhoek, arriving just in time for school on Monday morning.

He was sixteen at the time. Would modern-day Lotharios walk to Franschhoek for us girls? I wondered.

We had stopped in Beaufort West the evening before. Besides the car having a broken water pump, which was fixed only at 2 p.m., I had noticed a sore throat coming on: it was a bit scratchy. Oh no, I thought, I can't get ill now. It was not the time to get tonsillitis. We spent the next night in the Huguenot Hotel in Franschhoek, and there was no doubt I had a very sore throat and chest pains. They were still there when Monday, 23 June 1986, dawned rainy and cold.

We drove up towards the farm through steady rain. The huge Stuttaford's van had just arrived, and all was the usual hustle and bustle. 'Was this the right place? Gosh, what a drive to negotiate!'

The staff had appeared and they stood silently in the rain, without seeking shelter. There were three men as well as the wife of one of them, named Dinie. They were of middle height, with shiny brown eyes, and very respectful. We greeted each other, I in English and they in Afrikaans. I asked if they might help to unpack the furniture, but they stood and looked at me with no reaction. I asked them the same question again. They stood expressionless in the dripping rain, looking at nothing. I asked the woman, Dinie, why they didn't answer me. 'No, but merrim, you must speak Afrikaans,' she said.

Well, just dandy! Afrikaans was not the lingua franca of Johannesburg, and mine had only been in occasional use in the last thirty years. First lesson starts here, I thought as I scratched slowly through my vocabulary. The words came out hesitantly, but the men sprang to help us very willingly. My worldly goods came out of the pantechnikon and Stuttaford's left about six hours later.

The house was an absolute shambles. I had gone down to the village to buy buckets to catch the rainwater pouring through the roof. I asked Dinie to find the box marked 'Linen', and make up the now-erected beds for my father and myself, because certainly I was about to die. I rushed down to the shops again; three more leaks from the roof were spewing water onto the wooden floors and more buckets were needed to avert a flood inside the house. I went to the Co-op, bought food for three days, and collapsed into the freshly made-up bed.

It wasn't possible for me to get up for the next week or more. I was very ill, and as we had run out of food altogether, it seemed a good idea to give Dinie money to shop with. She came back with a bag of potatoes balanced on one shoulder and a bag of gem squash on the other. I had no interest in food and had given up eating altogether. I had already spent ten days in bed. To say I felt like the victim of the wrath of God was an understatement. Daddy looked rather mournful at the prospect of mealtimes. He was a vegetarian, but really this was a bit much!

Whatever I had was not going away, I knew no one, and had no telephone. One mid-afternoon, Daddy had been reading the Bible to me. The text was along the lines of full repentance and mortification of one's soul before breathing one's last, and I was giving a fair imitation of doing just that when we heard someone knocking on the kitchen door. Daddy went out to see who was there.

He came back with the news that there was a man to see me. 'Daddy, don't be ridiculous, I can't see anyone,' I whispered, croaking, and waved my arms feebly. He went to relay the message, and returned with Mr Christo Wheelbarrow, the manager of Boland Bank, through whom we had bought the farm. He was a nice-looking man, slender, with good refined hands, immaculate in his suit and carefully knotted tie, moustache trimmed to the last hair. He was a deacon of the church, as he had told me during our negotiations.

His first comments were most encouraging. 'My God, mevrou, jy lyk verskriklik,' he said. 'Was die dokter hier?' I explained the situation as best I could, and he rushed out of the door. Within fifteen minutes the doctor was in the room putting a stethoscope to my chest, taking my pulse and temperature. 'You are mad,' he said, 'you have double pneumonia. I'm giving you injections, pills, gargles and whatever, and I will be in tomorrow. Here is my phone number.'

I was just about to say, We don't have a phone, when Daddy heard knocking at the back door. Thanks to Christo, it was Bertie from the post office. A bedside phone was installed, plus another one in the study, and it was all done in half an hour. Ah, the benefits of small towns. My eternal gratitude to Bertie stems from that moment.

I phoned my sister in Johannesburg to tell her of my calamitous arrival. She said she thought we had died on the journey, not having heard a word from me. She then phoned my friend Annette in Cape Town, who phoned a friend in Paarl, who arrived three hours later with a huge pot of nourishing soup tasting of ambrosia, angels and damn fine chicken. Moreover, there was a three-day supply of it. Chicken soup is not called 'Jewish penicillin' for nothing.

Good food always makes me feel better, and within a day or two I was able to take a good look at the room in which I was lying. It had a high wooden ceiling and was well proportioned. There was a tall sash window in the west wall, with solid wooden shutters which fastened on the inside with a drop bolt. The window was facing the garden with a view down the Valley.

The room was too small, somehow, and since I had nothing better to do but lie and look at it, I wondered how it could be enlarged. Finally I saw that there was no cornice along the edge of the ceiling on the wall separating this bedroom from the next one. Hah! Some necessity for accommodation had persuaded someone in the past to divide a large bedroom into two smaller ones.

My son Peter, who was working in Cape Town, called each day to see if I had survived. He was visiting me the following weekend and bringing a friend or two. They were all competent cooks, so whether I was in or out of bed was irrelevant. In answer to his question whether he was going to get his inheritance prematurely, I said it seemed that I was recovering. We discussed times of arrival and what food he would bring, since my appetite was reasserting itself.

'That's all fine, Pete, but please, darling, also bring some hammers – you know, those big builder's ones, and some big chisels.'

I heard a note of exasperation in his voice. 'Ma, you are supposed to be dying; just what are you thinking of now?'

'Well, you see, there is this wall at the foot of the bed, and you know how easily I get claustrophobic, and I just lie here doing nothing and it bothers me. Just imagine how you would feel if you didn't do this for me, and I wasn't here any more.' I managed a theatrical sob. What's the point of having children if you can't resort to blackmail once in a while?

The three sturdy lads who arrived looked like a professional demolition team. They smashed the mud brick wall down on the Saturday, and on the Sunday they threw all the debris out of the windows onto the terrace, swept and dusted the entire room, vacuumed the walls and skirtings, washed windows, and scrubbed off the floor. Those old mud bricks had covered everything in fine red dust.

But I was returned to my bed with the wall now six metres away, everything smelling fresh and clean. By Monday afternoon the staff had taken all the rubble up to the municipal dump. The bedroom had instantly doubled in size, and one could see the gracious proportions which had originally been planned. There was only a bit of patching and a painting job left to do. That was my first renovation of the house.

I was still in bed, somewhat better, three days later, when Daddy says again, 'Gwen, there's a man to see you.'

'Daddy, I don't know any more men, and I look like hell. Please just take a message.'

The man departed, but left a bottle of wine and a small visiting card. It was from Michael Buchanan-Clarke, the first of the truly hospitable, helpful, kind and generous people whom I can never thank sufficiently for helping me make somewhat less of a fool of myself than I would otherwise have done.

I recovered under the doctor's ministrations, got the energy to get up and about, communicated with the staff more easily, and started farm life.

2

⟡

Farm Life Begins

Three weeks after arriving on the farm, recovered from pneumonia, I walked out of the house to take stock of what this farm was all about. It didn't look too promising. I was very warmly dressed, from spencer to anorak and waterproof boots. The ground was oozing water with every footstep, from the months of rain. It was midwinter, and snow sprinkled the mountains. The sky was a glacial blue; thin streaks of cloud were being pushed over the Drakenstein mountains by a south-westerly wind. The orchards in front of the house looked frostbitten and sad. Thick weeds in between the fruit trees were withered and dead. It was close to ploughing time, if it was not already overdue.

It was also the beginning of the pruning season, and a lot of people were in the orchards. I introduced myself to some women close to me. Asking about the cultivars, I found that most of the old favourites were no longer grown. The Early Dawns, tender white-fleshed peaches, luscious and slip-skinned, were too fragile to travel. The huge golden-yellow Kakamas cling peaches were familiar. These, I was told, all went down to the pack-shed to be tinned under a famous label and exported. Inspectors would come to the farm and tell me when to pick them. They did, and they also told me of the many deadly poisons I had to spray onto the fruit to protect the crop from fruit fly. I was appalled.

The Methley plums were unknown, so were Santa Rosa, but where were the satsumas? Thoughts of that wine-red flesh and juice in the Highveld made me swallow. They had been ripped out all over the surrounding valleys, as not commercially viable.

The planting on the farm consisted of one variety of peach and two kinds of plum. There were also two and a half hectares of chenin blanc grapes. We had a long pergola of hanepoots on the Transvaal farm, but wine grapes were new to me.

An extra 25 people had joined our small staff for the pruning season. These included older women and men, young men just out of school who had not found permanent work, and children free to do simple tasks during the holidays. The children were lively and thin, but looked as if growing was very hard work. Their facial expressions were too old for their bodies. They were wary, and stole their exuberance and laughter as if they were not entitled to it. They would put their hands across the lower half of their faces and duck their heads when they smiled, as if smiling was not approved. The part-timers would go from farm to farm, when the season started, for pruning, planting, and then harvesting. Since the farms had various cultivars which ripened at different times, they had steady employment most of the year.

I looked closely at everyone, almost all of whom were unknown to me. Very tall coloured people were not often seen in the Valley. Perhaps it was genetic predisposition: their ancestors had been the slight, fine-boned people from the East Indies. The genetic mix with the Dutch boers had lent a more muscular structure to their bodies. The men were of middle height, well proportioned, and with fine eyes, except for one of them. His eyes were hooded, and he never looked directly at me.

They were very respectful to me, but sensitive about their masculinity and rights. The slightest remark was measured to see if it might be an insult, then an aggressive reply would fly back. They put on a fine show of bravado to one another, but it was uncertain, and the women knew it. All their voices when they spoke to me were pitched at softer European tones, but they changed this to raucous loud speech with one another. There was, in some, the accent which is called a *bry*, which carries a rolled 'r' and is said to originate from Malmesbury, some eighty kilometres north-west of Cape Town. What was inherent in their behaviour was an exceptional and natural courtesy.

Many of the women were very thin. Others, the older ones, had put on a little weight. They held hands casually, as they walked along the rows, stroked each other's waists or shoulders with familiarity. They were not dressed warmly enough against the cold. The hunched shoulders and a tightness around their mouths revealed their hunger. Clothing was obviously 'hand-me-downs', mismatched and ill-fitting. They all wore a scarf around their heads, and it was in the colour, or in the angle of the bow when tying the scarf, that they suggested their individuality. Later on, I could identify them from a distance by the colour of their headgear, the colours rendered chalky in the hot sun.

Almost all of them had a robust and salty sexuality that reminded me of women I had seen living in Mediterranean ports. They were openly affectionate, challenging, inviting, quick to retort, and never at a loss for words. Strong men might find them an affront but could not afford to alienate them; to lesser men they were a threat as well as a lure. They mocked male weakness, and in such a small community they knew each other's weaknesses intimately. In colour they ranged from pale quince to coffee and light chocolate. Their faces were European. Here and there a lifted angle to the outer eye, or a slightly flattened cheekbone, told the story of their intercontinental journey. Occasionally there would be one face explicitly Oriental.

Then there was the matter of language. Afrikaans was the lingua franca of the Boland, although the younger people, recently schooled, spoke some English. It was word usage that intrigued and entertained me. Insults were part of the vocabulary. One particular word coloured everything they said. After some time working with the men, I concluded that they used 'fuck' as a noun, verb and an adjective. It was the expletive of choice. They would say to me, 'Merrim, give me that *fokken* pair of scissors' or, 'Where the *fok* are the vineyard cuttings?' The word infiltrated every verbal exchange: parents used it to children, and the children used it to their friends. Well, it had certainly been used from at least the sixteenth century, when the Scottish poet William Dunbar had written 'fukkit' in an amorous poem, still preserved in a collection of the songs of travelling lutenists in the Beineke Library at Yale.

It was much later that I realised how insidious the word had become. I was in the Co-op, bearded Billy behind the counter. His burly form and brusque manner belied a friendly nature. A number of the farmers were chatting idly while waiting to be served. Seeing me there, they said, 'Ladies first.' Billy asked me what I wanted. 'Just three metres of that fucking four-inch irrigation pipe, and two connectors. Andries ran the tractor over the pipe.' Billy looked at me. So did the other men, and they burst out laughing. 'Gwen, you need a holiday. You have been on the farm too long. You have been corrupted, it happens to everyone.'

It took me a moment to recall what I had just said. 'Oh goodness, I do apologise, Billy.' I was blushing.

'Don't worry, Gwen, we understand. By the way, do me a favour. When you come in here, put your make-up on first, please, I see enough men during the day. If you are the lady farmer, I would like to know you are still a woman.'

When I got home, I looked in the mirror. Billy certainly had a point.

❖

That morning I decided to concentrate on how a vine was pruned. It was men's work. They handled the vines with a gentleness almost reverential. Many of the women were pruning the trellised plums, but the men would not permit them to touch the vines. I wondered why, and I asked them. 'Nay, merrim, dis mans werk, hulle kom nie in die wingerd nie. Finish en klaar.' There was no particular reason given, but it was men's work, and that was that. I was puzzled.

Later that day I remembered something I had read in a book by Jane Grigson. She, being a much-published food writer, visited France from England at every opportunity. One particular visit was to gather material for an in-depth essay on the making of Roquefort cheese. At the entrance to the cave in which the Roquefort was maturing, she was stopped but her husband was allowed through. The male attendant asked her quietly, 'Avez-vous les règles?' As a fluent French speaker, she could hardly believe her ears. The man had asked her if she was menstruating! She was not, but asked him the reason for this personal question. 'Well you see, it can affect the cheese while it is maturing. It can also affect wine at a certain stage while it sleeps.'

'It will not be easy', Pliny the Elder (23–79 CE) wrote, 'to find anything with more miraculous effect than the menstrual blood of women. If they are in this condition and come in contact with new wine, it turns sour; at their touch the fruits of the field become unfruitful, grafts and cuttings wither away, seeds in the garden are parched and fruit falls from the tree under which a woman with her periods has sat.'

To find this belief still operative in a valley in Africa almost two thousand years later was astounding. I suspect it was brought to Franschhoek by the French Huguenots, some of whom arrived in 1683, with their knowledge of viticulture and the vine cuttings.

They had probably invoked all of God's blessings and used prayers, pagan rites and every other tradition or superstition possible to assist the new vines. Their future, in this wild country, depended on their vines growing and the wine being made. Back in France, persecution awaited. Not allowing women to touch the vines might, to them, have been a sensible precaution in this unknown environment. Just in case! Who knew what was in the air on the southern tip of the Dark Continent? Wine had never been produced here before, and maybe those suspicious Calvinistic Dutchmen who ran the Cape settlement might invoke some calamity or curse to put an end to their dreams.

I think the belief lingered in the Valley, but the reasoning had been lost. The Bible perpetuates this belief. The Israelite and Mesopotamian women were not permitted to sow any crops during their *menses* lest the seeds be contaminated. Many people in Africa share this tradition to this day. I liked the idea that a little paganism lingered in this hidden valley along with Bacchus and his acolytes.

I tried to imagine what my ancestor Jacques Pinard might have seen when his small party of Huguenot refugees arrived in Langebaan where they disembarked in the 1680s. They must have been thankful to have survived the journey, which took months in cramped unhygienic conditions, and see land again, however unfamiliar.

They were then given instructions by the Dutch to get their families together and start walking. Surrounding the bay, the flat land covered in various kinds of indigenous bush was totally different to home. Home had been Normandy, the moist, soft and luscious province in France, with grazing for sheep and for the cows that produce some of the best cheeses in the country.

As they moved further along, the soft hills gradually reared up into the edges of the Hex River mountains. They would soon have encountered animals: various types of antelope, lions, huge wild cats, elephants, wild pigs, a lot of snakes (many of them poisonous), and insects and spiders of all sizes and shapes. I heard that the last elephant was shot in the Valley by Koos 'Kallie' Hugo in 1863. He was a farmer and the elephant was pulling up his fruit trees. The elephants used to come to the Valley in summer, and in winter go up to Villiersdorp and across to Worcester.

Only nine or ten families were sent into the Valley, the same number were settled in Simondium, 21 were settled in Groot Drakenstein, more at the foot of Paarl Mountain, and some at Wamakerskamp on the edge of Wellington, as it is known today. The Dutch were not sympathetic and wanted them to be fully integrated as soon as possible. They wanted no sedition in their colony, and viewed these newcomers as a burden. The Huguenots were given slight help.

They were insular, as many persecuted people would be. The comfort of their language, and religious beliefs long fought for, probably made them oversensitive. They asked for French teachers for their children, and separate schools and churches, which were denied.

They had no transport, so could not keep contact with other families except in their immediate area. After one generation their children had lost their language. They were mixed in with the Dutch children, and that was the end of French as a learning medium at school. ❖

I asked Michael Buchanan-Clarke how I could learn more about vines. He recommended a book, which I bought and started reading. Armed with some understanding, I joined the men a week later, book in hand. Curiously, they did not object to my pruning the vines, and seemed delighted to help me and gave lots of advice. They wanted to see the pictures in the book, and compare what they had been taught with this new source of information. They voiced their opinions. It was useful to see how methods of pruning varied.

The children still on holiday and many women were involved

in the labour of *stokkies optel*. Women walked in between the rows of trees, and, using a rake or their hands, gathered all the clippings into piles. Another woman collected the little piles and carried them to the end of the rows. It was fairly labour-intensive. Yet more women, or adolescent boys, picked up the much larger piles of cuttings at the ends of the rows, then put them into bins on the tractors. They had done the work for so long, communication was wordless.

The weather was bright but bitterly cold and I saw that many of the labourers drank only water at lunchtime. I asked Dinie why they didn't bring some lunch to work. 'They don't have any money, merrim, and they have children,' she said by way of explanation. The children had to be fed before any others.

I had noticed that when the conversation turned to the poverty in the Valley, or the conditions of employment on some of the farms, which they named, there was no criticism of the farmers. Do poor people like these stimulate our sense of living by putting before our eyes their daily struggle for existence? Poverty is always humiliating. It forces you to live someone else's view of your own life. They suffered silently, and were embarrassed by their inability to defend themselves or to make demands on people that a number of them really did believe were superior. Anyway, jobs were too precious to forfeit by complaining.

Because of my pneumonia, Bill, still in Johannesburg, had made an arrangement with the previous owner to pay the staff weekly until I recovered. What was not discussed but taken for granted was that it would be on the same basis as he had paid them previously; but the amount paid to each person had not been checked, nor had the hourly rate. Cash cheques had been written out to cover the quoted costs.

On a particularly cold Saturday morning, rain was sweeping down the Valley. Knocking on the kitchen door was unusual but it happened that day, so I went to see who it was. Andries, the spokesman on the farm, was there with a small group of women. I asked him what he wanted.

'Merrim,' he said, 'these people were not paid. Master is now gone for a weekend. Hulle het nie kos nie.'

'But why didn't you tell me earlier, Andries? The bank is closed. How much money do they get?'

They stood huddled in the rain, eyes downcast. I knew the casuals were paid on a daily basis.

'Is nine rand, merrim, for each.'

'Yes, but how many days did they work?'

'Merrim, this week, three days.'

'So then that is twenty-seven rand each.'

'Nay, merrim, is nine rand.'

They were working eight hours a day, for three rands a day. I looked at these women, and felt the bitterest shame I could remember.

I know all the arguments for this kind of abuse. There are so many who justify it by pointing out that it is three rands they didn't have before. That much is true. What is also true is that it merely took a longer time for them to become seriously ill and physically undermined. Food was the only area where they could cut costs. Poverty, alcoholism and tuberculosis stalked these valleys; unbeknown to me, two of my staff already had TB.

My next emotion was absolute, murderous fury. That bastard, with his smarmy manners, had been abusing his staff for years. He was a pillar of the church, he went to the prayer meetings each week. He was university-educated, at Stellenbosch. I wanted to kill him with my bare hands.

'Come into the kitchen, all of you, and Grandpa will make you coffee and sandwiches. I will go and get some money.'

They wouldn't come in, because they would drip water onto the kitchen floor. I had to threaten them that if they didn't come in out of the rain, they wouldn't get their money. They were fed and paid.

I told Andries there would be a meeting on Monday morning.

23

The day came, and the staff, casuals included, gathered around me. I told them that I had been unaware of the previous owner's conduct, and that with immediate effect the wages would be raised. I told them that if he set foot on my property ever again they must call me and I would shoot him. I phoned him and told him the same thing. The atmosphere on the farm lifted from that day.

I decided to give all the labourers a hot lunch. Dinie pulled out my huge jam pots from the back of a cupboard, and I considered how to feed thirty people on a daily basis for several weeks. It had to be a filling meal, nourishing and economical. I drove off to Paarl after picking up some few groceries in the village, to see if the shopping there might be cheaper.

I went to the Paarl Co-op and walked alongside the shelves to see which supplies might fit the bill. I saw that day-old bread was less than half price, and mostly fed to chickens and pigs. I bought it all as well as sacks of dried beans, peas, samp, barley, lentils, corn and rice, huge tins of veggies discounted for some reason, and elderly cabbages and carrots at bargain prices. Packets of soup made a contribution to taste when mixed with everything else, and so did Marmite and Oxo.

I spent an evening weighing things out with Daddy's help. It seemed that I could give everyone a soup bowl of 'stew' at a cost of 35 cents per plate. The bread, smeared with garlic and oil, was given a new lease of life. Heated in the oven, it was gobbled up.

Dinie and I carried out the huge pots on the first day. She was my maid and had helped me cook, so she dished up. People came timidly at first, and told me that they had never been given a hot lunch during working hours. It was plain but tasty and sustaining, and well worth the effort; and the gratitude was overwhelming. Later the women would ask, 'En wat kry ons vandag, Miz Gwen?' Some of the mixtures became favourites.

The lunches were the most incredible attraction. Oumas tottered up the hill to do a little this or that, and left after lunch. They were all family; I simply didn't care if there were a few extra mouths to feed. Fridays became chicken days. They were a reward for the week's work. There was a chicken farm not far away. They were generous with the chickens and the price when they heard who were being fed. Dinie did a head count half an hour before lunch, and if necessary we could stir in two or three extra cups of rice to make it all go further. Some days it was like the story of the loaves and fishes, but miraculously everyone got something to eat.

❖

Saturdays and Sundays were for recovering from Friday nights, for relaxing, visiting, and church attendance. In the white church, the Dutch Reformed congregation dressed soberly out of respect for their Lord. The men's clothing, their uniform of dark suits, dark polished shoes, plain ties and plain shirts, was suited to the sober expressions they wore.

The women wore their church hats, stockings, girdles and dresses in darkish colours with sleeves, as sleeveless dresses would offend the older members of the congregation. They also wore pious expressions with their eyes downcast, absorbing spiritual nourishment.

However, having done the same thing myself at my father's church, I knew that behind those expressions some of the ladies were harbouring thoughts of a different nature and of more immediate nourishment. Some of them were thinking about the Sunday lunch. One was thinking of the fish her son had caught last evening at the Strand beach, and she was probably going over the recipe she had used for a new sauce as a special treat for Dominee and the new neighbours at lunch. Another might be considering if she had put enough parsley and thyme in the stuffing for the Sunday duck or chicken that was to welcome her daughter's prospective in-laws. Would the napkins have enough starch in them for the creases to have been ironed knife-sharp? Was the oven the right temperature to leave the roast unattended for so long? Was the new ice-cream recipe with condensed milk in it really going to fall out of the round mould looking 'just like the breast of a virgin', as Aunty Franny had said it would. Aunty Franny thought that putting a glacé cherry on the top like a nipple was an unnecessary depravity and might give the adolescents inappropriate ideas.

After the service the farmers and their steadfast good women stood in the garden, shook hands with Dominee, and exchanged greetings with friends and neighbours. Then they went home to prepare for lunch.

The other church, the one the coloured farm workers went to, was more lively. There was much singing of songs, with spontaneous soprano solos sung in between the verses of traditional hymns. Little girls were starched, pinafored, scrubbed and beribboned with hair bows bigger than their faces. They were very much aware of being on show, the pride of their mothers, who had made their dresses and ribbons, knitted their socks, and given them their manners. Older girls moved more languidly, pushing their new breasts before them and sliding their legs forward in a walk that was absolutely thrilling to the boys, watching either from the back or the front. *Jirre*, man, it was worth coming to church for this display of fresh-scrubbed womanhood. Somehow school uniforms just didn't make them look like they looked in a pair of stretch jeans and a tight top. This kept many minds occupied.

If Dominee went on too long, whispered conversations went on in the back pews, tips for the horse races at Milnerton were passed on, where to get good school clothing at a discounted price, and who had a special on fish for the weekend. The odd hip flask went around to relieve the headache of the day before. Sometimes when Dominee got a bit too heavy about eternal damnation, you had to take notice, just in case on your deathbed you had to confess properly. But deathbeds were not in mind for the younger folk – there was too much to live for.

The women were splendid in brightly coloured frocks and headgear, from the traditional scarf to turbans, sunbonnets and proper hats. Oumas who had succumbed to the heat and were snoring loudly were wakened gently and led out into the vestibule. Nursing mothers stayed put and fed their babies where they were. Small boys were sometimes pinioned to their seats for the last ten minutes, and as the final hymn faded they flew outside, their thin bodies all sharp angles with energy, like low-flying kites, to be the first in line for the games and refreshments to follow.

When church was over there was much to do. There was a lively trade in poultry, including ducks, fancy bantams and the occasional set of racing pigeons. You didn't buy those until you had their pedigree and athletic results in the last three races certified. Tante Rosa sold her very special ginger beer. Dominee did a lively trade in his new hybrid begonias, and the *smous* had picked up some cheap fencing poles and chicken wire, which were all sold in a minute. Ouma Bester made aniseed rusks that reminded everyone of their mothers', and her watermelon *konfyt*, man, it was the best, it still had a crunch under your teeth, and was tingly sweet from the bits of ginger and lemon rind she added. The children rushed about screaming with delight at being alive, and whether they were barefoot or shod it made no difference, as one poor mother said, for God loves everybody, especially children.

Going down the hill to the village to buy the Sunday newspapers in the morning, I was amazed that the coloured families presented quite such a splendid picture as they paraded down the main street to their church. Most of the staff housing provided at that time was rudimentary. Indoor sanitation was not a norm, electricity was not always provided, and storage space in the tiny houses was minimal. Yet everything they wore was spotlessly clean, pressed, starched and polished. And the walk to church was indeed a parade, largely in the hands of the women. It displayed to the village that one had a husband who was sober, God-fearing, a good provider, who cared about his family and was a respected member of the community.

Sundays, later in the afternoon, were also washdays for the farmworker families, as most of the women worked from Mondays to Fridays. The laundry was hung over fences, rambling roses and shrubs, and festooned the sides of the roads all the way down to the last farm before the highway. It showed exactly who lived in each cottage. A fresh line of nappies told of another addition to the family. Rugby jerseys, school shirts, aprons, work clothes, various bits of underwear, bedding, towels and dishcloths spoke of the family's housekeeping. In November, when the dog roses covered every fence all over the Boland, the white of the roses and bits of brightly coloured washing flung over them looked like the aftermath of a bridal party. When it rained for days at a time, the washing stayed outside until the sun came out again.

And then there was the fact of trust in the Valley. No one's laundry was ever stolen. I stayed there for years and heard of only one case, where the thief was so incompetent that she wore someone's new blouse down to the village and it was snatched back by the irate owner, who happened to pass her in the middle of the street. The culprit walked home in skirt and bra. Most regrettably it is no longer possible to be so trusting.

Slowly I got to know everyone, coloured and white. They became individuals. The names, relationships and links to each other became a pattern I could follow. I asked where they lived and where they had originally come from. Six or eight generations of history could be rattled off without hesitation.

Many people born in the Valley had never left. They knew the soil and the seasons, the winds and the rains, and they could smell a change in the weather three hours before it happened. They said that frost smelt of Dettol and sometimes of smoke. They said that the smell of honey blew in from the hills before the strong, hot winds of October, which turned everything it touched to rust.

The strong north-west wind, blowing the heavy winter rains down the Valley, smelt of old fish and boats, they said. Yes, I thought, and of the ports that sheltered them, the women waiting at the edges of the sea, of shifting continents, of dreams and illusions, forgotten lovers, and of dying. It was a melancholy season.

The coloured people of the Valley had lived on the farms with the same Huguenot families for generation after generation. They lay buried together, master and servant, in the family graveyards. Perhaps then, laid to rest, they journeyed back in ethereal form to their islands perfumed with tamarisk, incense and spices.

Life was changing in the valleys, slowly then, but with increasing swiftness. Franschhoek was about to be discovered, and these days would be no more.

3

⤭

The Penitent

Once one has turned right at the end of the Valley just before the bridge, crossed the railway line and passed the sawmill, the road from Franschhoek to Paarl lies straight through another valley with hills running parallel to it on the right-hand side.

It was along this stretch of road that I first saw the man I called St Paul. He was a tall man, a giant in fact, who had shrunk over the years. I knew instantly that he was ancient, older than the whole world, but he was still massive in the shoulders, heavy in his trunk like a long-lived tree, with thickly muscled legs and powerful arms. Across his chest and over his shoulders was a heavy harness that might once have been used on a team of horses, pulling a low cart on small wheels. The cart had streamers of wire of varying lengths attached to it, some perhaps six metres long, which trailed motley articles behind him.

They might have looked like a variation of the 'Just Married' debris attached to the honeymoon car, except for their incongruity. A wrecked baby's pram was crammed full of unhinged toilet seats. Another wire pulled several broken spades and rakes, which constantly impeded his progress by catching in clumps of weeds. An old kettle bounced behind the remains of a vacuum cleaner pipe. Other wires dragged the scuffed remains of a pink boned surgical corset, the dried-out thigh bone of an ox, a bicycle tyre without the wheel, the battered remains of a caned headboard for a single bed, and a plastic woven sack full of turnips and cabbages. All the connecting wires were festooned with plastic bags, tied in knots for decoration.

In the small cart itself, he carried the essentials for his existence. I knew that they meant little to him; he was a biblical penitent who had set the parameters of his penances himself, and therefore they would be inviolate. It seemed that St Paul, moving along his own personal road to Damascus, had condemned himself to walk forever, dragging his penances in any weather until time, his or the world's, finally stood still.

I asked in the Valley about him, but there was little information. He was from north-west Africa, someone thought, and had, after a brutal fight in which he might have killed a man, sustained some damage to his mind or his soul. His chosen route embraced Malmesbury, Wellington, Paarl, Franschhoek, Villiersdorp, Worcester, and sometimes in spring he was reported to be seen at Langebaan lying for days in the glorious profusion of indigenous spring flowers. I was touched to hear that he allowed himself this innocent indulgence.

He would appear along the roads near Franschhoek with his burdens every six weeks or so. After that first sighting I saw him regularly if not often, and he looked absolutely the same, in clothing, expression and purpose. The glacial evangelical fervour of the saint after whom I had called him was gleaming in his eyes, and his face was isolated from human enquiry and contact.

Once I left a bag food for him which I had in the car, about 150 metres ahead of him on his path. I saw him pick it up. After this and years of random sightings, I did not see him again. His journey had been completed.

4

❧❧❧

Season of the Snails

In early September there was real sun again, with some warmth in it. The warmth had brought the blossoms popping out overnight. A pink and white froth appeared on the trees, gorgeous to behold. The ploughed soil between the vines and the trees erupted into a yellow carpet of oxalis, pink gaura and weeds. In the flower gardens, roses put out their first tender shoots, lavender showed the first delicate grey spokes of new leaves. Insects of all kinds arrived, making their own kind of music. The earth was fertile and ripe for birth – creation was come again.

Daddy was the general dogsbody. He was eighty years old when we arrived in Franschhoek and still a handsome man. His hair, snow white, was thick and wavy, and he had a swarthy skin, a legacy of Spanish wrecks on the Cornish coast.

No islands in the world are more treacherous or have a more fearful history than the Scillies. Entire lists of maritime casualties on the south-west coast of Cornwall carry the awful words 'Struck, Struck, Struck'. The choice for young Spaniards washed ashore was murder or marriage. Since men from Cornwall were also victims of wrecks, virile young men were in short supply. Father was quite clearly the product of the second option. He had navy blue eyes, an aquiline nose, the posture of a prince, and everyone spoke of his good manners and grace.

He was repairing the house on a room-by-room basis, patiently finishing one thing before he started another. Little Farm, or Patrysfontein, as the farm was also called, was 120 years old. Elderly shutters, hanging off their hinges, needed attention. Daddy was building cupboards in all the bedrooms and shelving in the temporary kitchen. It had been temporary for the previous eighty years, and was the last word in inconvenience.

The one usable bathroom had a bath sunk right into the floor. One had to crawl on hands and knees on the floor and slide into it. Daddy declared it was far too undignified for a man of his age to do this. In preference he stood half-frozen under the cold-water shower, calling out 'Very fresh!' to me when he came out from under it with teeth chattering.

His rituals were his security. First thing in the morning, he read his Bible for half an hour, then brought rooibos tea to my bedroom and we chatted for a while before I got up. His mornings were for pottering. He conversed with the owls, and the owls hooted back. The air was fresh and fragrant with the light perfume of blossoms. He picked the CMR beetles off the rose bushes. They went into a bucket that contained paraffin, there to have a rapid death. The beetles were an easy target, dressed in their gaudy black and yellow carapaces – the regimental colours of the Cape Mounted Rifles that gave them their 'CMR' name. These were pastimes suitable for an elderly gentleman.

34

One morning, he came to call me most urgently. 'Gwen, come quickly, you won't believe your eyes.' I didn't believe my eyes, and I was speechless. The entire front walls of the house were thick with snails. They had left their slimy trails all the way up to the gutters.

They were in legions, traversing the lawn and being crunched underfoot, climbing through open windows, and demolishing everything green and juicy in the garden. New battalions were getting their marching orders from guerrillas in the surrounding fields. This was a serious invasion, and immediate action was called for.

The buckets, previously purchased for collecting the rainwater spewing inside the house, now did duty as containers for snails. Thickly sprinkled with salt, the snails came to a very sticky end. In spite of my telling the staff that this was part of a spring diet in France and that snails were meat, they were having none of it. Neither was I, having always hated them.

The Oumas and anyone else without chores were pressed into service. Their instruction was: 'Kill every one of the buggers.' I fetched dozens of sacks of snail bait from the Co-op. Billy, in charge of the Co-op, kept score. One large estate further down the Valley was already counting bags of bait by the thousand. The Co-op had to order extraordinary quantities of pellets.

We poured the bait in a huge semicircle along the road that divided the orchards from the house. Each morning the trail of pellets was dense with bodies and shells. It looked like a tide line on the beach where the lighter shells come to rest. Those snails that had survived were collected by hand off every plant in the garden, the walls, gutters, window ledges, rooms and even my bed. Daddy found a copulating couple in his slippers.

The newspapers printed pictures of some enterprising estate owners trucking their flocks of ducks and geese around the vineyards to eat the snails. They rented the flocks out on a daily basis to adjoining farms. A wide plank was rested on the open end of the bakkie, and there the geese walked down, two by two, just as if they were leaving the Ark. Prized champion snail-eaters were awarded a red ribbon to wear around their necks, and had their photographs on the front page of the *Cape Times*. It was a change from the usual boring politicians, and the geese were more photogenic. Competitions developed from farm to farm, as to which goose was the true Boland champion. Statistics of how many millions of snails had arrived that season were printed daily, along with extraordinary remedies for their instant demise.

This plague continued for six weeks. It was all blamed on the weather and changing temperatures. Then one day it stopped. There was not one snail to be found anywhere. Caution prevailed for a few days, and we knew it was over.

Why wasn't everyone eating them, or exporting them to France? 'Nee sies, merrim, ons eet dit nie!' was my workers' opinion. I'd asked the restaurant owners why they didn't cash in on this unexpected windfall. 'Mostly, Gwen, I don't think they fall into the category of *boerekos*,' I was told by one of the locals. 'We don't want to lose the customers we've got. It's getting competitive in this small town.' Prophetic words!

5

The Carpenter

The rain poured down for more weeks at a time, and through the roof in several places at once. The house was just over a hundred years old, and repairs had been kept to a minimum by the previous owners. I asked around for a handyman. Someone knocked on the kitchen door.

There stood a dark-haired man with an unblemished olive skin and thick wavy hair that fell past his shoulders. He had a full beard, which hung to his chest. His eyes were dark brown and fringed with exceptionally long lashes. His expression was of one bearing an ancient, unfairly inflicted wound, carried without reproach. He bore a striking resemblance to Jesus before he went blond, as depicted in northern European medieval paintings. I have been to

Oberammergau and seen photographs of the various Christs who have participated in the Passion play through the decades. If the producers had seen this man first, he would have been their only choice for the starring role. Dinie and I almost genuflected.

'Môre, merrim,' he said, 'I hear you were looking for a carpenter and handyman, so I come to see you.' His demeanour was that of someone out of time past. There was an elegance and courtesy about him that I have rarely seen. I asked him to come in, to show him what was needed and see whether the job I had in mind, and his skills, were compatible. After the discussion and cups of coffee, I decided to employ him. I asked the *volk* to enquire about him over the weekend. His name was Wessel. 'Nay, merrim,' they said on Monday, 'he doesn't come from here, niemand weet van hom.'

Wessel arrived promptly that morning, with a toolbox on the back of a bicycle. After several hours on the roof, there was far less water dripping into the strategically placed buckets. He knew what he was doing. An hour later he had stopped all the leaks. What to do next in the way of improvements?

In the dining-room there was a flying chimney. Many years before, a *stoof* had stood beneath it, but now the stove had been removed and the chimney was an obstacle to moving round the end of the dining-room table. We were always banging our heads on it, which caused more grief than a hangover. I suggested to Wessel that if he used a chisel and chipped carefully, we could get the chimney off the wall without too much damage. A bit of plastering over the ragged edges, and all would be well.

A few hours of careful chipping followed. I was out on the veranda when there was the most awful crash and the sounds of collapsing masonry. I rushed to the dining-room.

Technically, it was no longer a room, as one entire wall was lying in heaps of bricks on the floor, and I was looking out into the garden. Wessel – unharmed, thank goodness – was standing gobsmacked, gaping at the result of his handiwork.

'O Jirre, merrim, ek is jammer, ek het dit nie gedoen, merrim, I was so very careful,' he spluttered. Tears were running down his thin face.

'Wessel, I know you were careful, it's not your fault, there must be an explanation,' I said. I wanted to apologise to him – somehow it wasn't fair that this accident had happened to him.

The cold air and rain were now blowing into the heart of the house. We shut all the doors we could, made up a pot of strong coffee, poured in a tot of KWV five-year-old brandy, then drank it down as remedy against the cold and shock.

Suitably fortified, we went to look at the other side of the wall along the ceiling line, which the house beams had prevented from falling down. There was the answer. It was the result of someone taking a shortcut many, many seasons ago. Someone, and I had names for him, had been short of a length of pipe. The downpipe from the gutter had been spied, removed and never replaced. The outside paint and plaster had not been maintained. All the water gushing against the wall from a four-inch gap in the guttering had found cracks and fissures to soak into. Gradually the old mud brick wall turned back into mud. All it required was a bit of banging, and hey presto! Better than with the Big Bad Wolf, the wall came tumbling down.

Well, this boer also had to *maak 'n plan*, and some alternative arrangements were made almost at once. I drew up a diagram, showed it to the chaps in the village, who approved it all, and we got started immediately. A lovely addition was made, with a spacious dining-room and an artist's studio for Bill's forays into reproducing the paintings of Gauguin, for which he had found an extraordinary talent. I had asked him to make me one, and the result was virtually museum quality. We stopped short of any further flying chimneys.

Wessel became a fixture on the farm. He kept entirely to himself at lunchtime and tea breaks, and he spoke little. He had the creative imagination required for a craftsman. I needed some retaining walls to terrace the new garden. We stretched out the hose and moved it into graceful looped patterns for the new shrubberies. He needed a thick piece of wood to measure one part of it, which was to be stepped down to the lawn, and I told him to go round the back of the house where he would find some big planks.

He came back from around a corner that was deeply shaded, towards me. He was sweating and bent forward under a huge wooden beam, and was straining under the weight. He lifted his head, and looked at me with his great sad eyes. I was once again in Jerusalem, on the Via Dolorosa. Angry and emotional crowds were around us, pushing and shouting. The drawn face, the wounded eyes and long hair were eerily identical to all of the representations down history: Christ to be crucified, in full knowledge and acceptance of his fate. Did I dream that, in the distance, I heard a cock crowing?

I turned away, and went to fetch a jug of cold water. We sat in the garden in silence. He looked at me for a long time, but never spoke. I sent him home because I couldn't have been in his presence again that afternoon. It was too disturbing, and irrationally made me want to cry out loud at the injustice that had taken place.

Over time, he built a series of stone walls, beautifully crafted, the stones carefully selected for colour and shape. Other walls were plastered, and steps designed. This work was done with the true hands of an ancient craftsman. His manners and behaviour never altered. Punctual, prepared, quiet, attentive to the task, he was enveloped in the grace and serenity of knowing his worth. It was above rubies.

I had the feeling that he never forgave that wall for collapsing. He remarked on it quietly, but often. It was a blot on his immaculate career. Once he had finished all our work, I recommended him to many other people in the village. There had been telephone numbers to call. They remained unmade, and no one ever saw him again. He vanished as if he had never been, and yet his presence has remained with me. I have seen him on crosses and paintings, in churches everywhere. His image is eternal. I always recognise his eyes.

❖

Some of the greatest expressions down history of man's creativity, along with music, art, churches, sculpture, architecture, gardens and buildings, are in cabinet-making. These men are dignified, quiet, painstaking, and devoted to their craft. They run their hands down the grain of woods gathered from distant forests, with the same patience and delicacy of touch they might use to quieten a child or love a woman. The nephew of the Queen of England calls himself a carpenter. The history of the great houses of the world, and all varieties of family homes, would be bleak without the astonishing staircases, doorways, ceilings, panelling and furniture, cupboards and shelves, tables, chairs and beds which still dominate our definition of home.

My family ancestor Jacques Pinard was a carpenter. My father was a carpenter who made furniture, and my niece, an architect in Alaska, is married to a cabinet-maker.

6

The Deelkas

The original deeds of Patrysfontein show a much larger portion of land than we had bought. It had been subdivided several times. Above the Pass Road it stretched up to a beautiful stream. This was the farm's water supply, and had been so for a hundred years or more. When the upper part was put on separate title, that portion also shared the water. Unbeknown to me, it also supplied some of the municipal water.

In 1986 it rained and rained! Goodness me, and in winter too. Newly arrived from the arid Transvaal, I thought it rained for a month without stopping. We were not used to this up in Jo'burg. No wonder the Cape people didn't think as fast as us. Their brains were waterlogged.

Our dam filled very slowly, but I noticed that the municipality's dam was spilling over. I didn't make the connection. Some time later I mentioned it to an old hand in the village who seemed to know what was going on. 'Go to the municipal office, Gwen, and complain. I think it's something to do with the *deelkas*.'

I did that, and was informed that I should meet the municipal officer on the Pass Road above my farm the following day at 10 a.m. I was waiting there when a small bakkie arrived. A man stepped out and introduced himself. His name was Sannie. He was of average height, pleasant to look at, and very well groomed – dark hair plastered with Brylcreme, shoes polished, safari suit pressed, comb in his knee-length socks. He listened attentively while I voiced my concerns.

'Ja, môre, meisie, follow me and we will see what goes on,' he said, and started up the hill. There was no path, and loose gravel, bushes, trees and boulders didn't help, but up we went. He was faster than I was, it got steeper and bushier, and several times I lost him. At last we arrived at the *deelkas*. I had never seen one before.

It was a concrete box built into the earth, with two pipes leading out of the sides opposite each other. Another bigger pipe from the hillside led water into the top of the *deelkas* from the spring. One of the side pipes, he pointed out, was for the municipality's water supply, and the other was to our farm. What entertained me was a Pick 'n Pay bag closing the mouth of one of the water pipes. He explained that all one had to do was put the bag onto the other pipe, and regularly change them round. He untied the bag, put it onto the other pipe, and I heard the water gurgling down the pipe to my dam.

'You see, this is all you have to do. If we forget, just come and change the bag from one pipe to the other.' Well, talk of technology! That practical job fell to my father, of course, and he loved it. He walked up the mountain each morning, remembering school picnics that had happened 65 years before. He checked the water level of the dam. This might be the day for another visit up the hill to the *deelkas* to change the Pick 'n Pay bag from our pipe to the municipality's, or vice versa.

Sannie and I walked back down the hill. We said our goodbyes but he turned to me again.

'Jirre, meisie, as ek na jou kyk, kry ek 'n kielie in my lies.' I didn't want to know about his *kielie* and walked firmly down the farm road.

When both dams were full, the overflow water gushed down the mountain, under the Pass Road, into a storm-water pipe, partly down our farm road, down a huge sloot, and ended up in the Berg River, usually taking part of our road with it. It was an unreliable water supply. Years later, it became much more so when the mania for bottled water arrived. The original source for the first 'Franschhoek Bottled Water' was this stream, which also supplied my bath water.

7

The Borehole Specialist

My partner, Bill, decided we should perhaps look into sinking a
borehole. Arrangements were made with some technical-sounding
department at Stellenbosch University. A man phoned to make an
appointment. He was to be there at 11 a.m. next Wednesday. On
time, a battered bakkie arrived at the house. A man, rounded and
friendly, with rumpled sandy hair and smiling blue eyes, got out of
the bakkie and introduced himself. He was dressed for walking, in
sweater, corduroys, anorak and sturdy shoes. He was the sort of
chap your mother would trust to bring you home unmolested and
on time.

All the usual pleasantries were exchanged. 'What a wonderful
view you have from this hill, you are so lucky not to be in Johan-

nesburg any longer, free of all that traffic and crime, a different lifestyle, lovely people, much more relaxed.'

'Would you like to have tea?' I asked.

Well, our visitor couldn't think of anything in the world that would be better. We went into the sitting-room, where he settled comfortably on the sofa, feet up on a footstool, his hands folded across his little belly. I brought the tea through, and served it with a plate of biscuits.

He had two cups of tea and ate almost all the biscuits. He and Bill were involved in a discussion of Robbie Burns's poetry, so books were fetched for reference. I went out to plant some seedlings with Martin, the gardener. After we were all done, half an hour later, I went back to the house. I found Bill and the bore-hole specialist discussing the early works of Beethoven. They were listening to CD renditions by various conductors.

Both of them had their eyes closed, and Bill was waving the fly-swatter in time to the music. I went off to the kitchen to think about lunch. I knew we would be having a guest, and it was already 12.15.

There was fresh trout from John on the hill, and mustard dill sauce to go with it, and guacamole done that morning. I had made buckwheat crêpes with spinach and ricotta. All the things for salad were in the vegetable garden. Half of an onion shortbread was left from supper the night before. Was this enough? This jolly fellow was clearly an accomplished eater. I opted for some delicious cheeses, especially the Roquefort and the soft Camembert bought in from Ludwig at La Cotte the day before. Bread is not the staff of life; it is the crutch of my existence. We were well supplied. Perhaps adding a risotto with fennel would fill up any empty corners. Our plums stewed in red wine would do for dessert, with fresh cream.

I took a peep into the sitting-room. There was an atlas on the floor. The visitor had a relative who had recently relocated to the wilds of Yorkshire. My partner grew up there, so they had to find the exact village. Was it near Lake Windermere and John Tovey, the famous cook, or closer to the moors on the east side? Bill's grandfather and father were engineers, setting up cotton mills in Yorkshire and India. Long discussions on the history of the cotton mills followed. Cotton led to speaking of India. There were relatives in India, but which part of India? The page was found in the atlas. Was it near the Ganges or in Kashmir?

Which were Bill's and his father's regiments? British regiments in England or India were then compared. Had his father been in Hodson's Horse? Were the 17th 21st Lancers more illustrious than the Bengal Lancers? Bill responded to this particular mention. Military service was compulsory in Britian after the War. Bill had been interviewed for the 17th 21st by a brigadier. The questions which particularly charmed him were: How much was his private income at the time? and How many of his own mounts would he be bringing? The answer was a loud zero, but he had prospects. That didn't quite cut it with this particular regiment.

By 1.30 I got them to the lunch table. Oh, the lunch was wonderful, the man said. Bill had opened several bottles of wine for his delectation. He had two helpings of everything and was looking around the table for more. Glasses were clinked. Each wine was pronounced better than the last.

The cheeses were served, and my goodness, one couldn't eat such superb examples of the French cheesemakers' art without … um, a decent port. An eyebrow was raised. Bill leapt up and produced the decent port. The guest couldn't decide if that little Brie from Normandy via Ludwig, an importer of scrumptious cheeses in the village, was better than the French Camembert. He would most regretfully just have a little slice more of both, then he could decide. I was mesmerised. I had never seen anyone eat so much.

I made a comment about a new recording of Mahler conducted by an American businessman. This particular chap had made Mahler his retirement project. He had recently left the New York

47

stock exchange after making millions of dollars, and had always passionately wanted to conduct Mahler's works. He could now afford to; he could actually afford his own orchestra, in fact. I was verbally attacked by Bill and Stellenbosch's answer to Robert Carrier. 'That dilettante, that, that American! He couldn't conduct a primary school choir, never mind his arrogance in starting on the Cleveland Philharmonic. My God, did he have to bring the violins in so abruptly, without a suitable pause? And what had he done about the cellos? Just forgot them – they had to find their own way in. And his body gyrations when he conducted! Who did he think he was, Furtwängler or Toscanini? He deserved to end up in the orchestra pit!'

At 4 p.m. they were still talking, with no mention of the purpose of the visit. I suggested that perhaps the borehole specialist could walk around on the farm and decide on a suitable location, waterwise. 'Oh, my dear,' he said, 'I am afraid that is out of the question. I haven't had such a good time in years, and I couldn't possibly concentrate on what I was doing. I think I have had a little too much to drink. I will have to come again.' Rather shakily, he left.

'Well, wasn't he just the best company, such a dear chap,' said Bill enthusiastically. I reminded him of the purpose of the man's visit. 'Gosh,' he said, 'I forgot about the borehole. I thought he was a friend of yours.'

A week later, the next appointment drew near and was upon us. I made sure that when the specialist arrived he just had time to get out of his bakkie, and within minutes I had the staff haul all his equipment off the back, sling it over their shoulders, and assume the attitude of Sherpa porters ready to take Hillary up Everest. I did not invite him into the house. He had tea and a sandwich sitting on a wall under the oak tree. Later he declared he had found the perfect spot that would yield 20 000 gallons an hour. It was right inside the slope of our dam wall.

We got a second opinion. We decided on the second opinion's

opinion and got 8000 gallons an hour, which was certainly enough for our needs. I came to the conclusion that the man who had come to lunch availed himself of generous farm hospitality all over the Boland. He could have written a comprehensive *Guide Michelin* on the area.

8

❧❀❧

The Owls of Patrysfontein

I had been in Franschhoek for some months before I heard the owls. I was always in the kitchen at dusk, making supper for my father and myself. I used to play vocal games to see how close I could get to imitating them. Daddy joined in. Over time the owls – there were several of them – took up residence in a large gum tree in the back yard. So we, Daddy and I, had our conversations with them each evening. Surprisingly, they began to respond, and it was part of the evening ritual to talk to the owls.

One evening, after Daddy had returned to Johannesburg for a spell and I had deposited my partner, Bill, at the airport, I decided to weed the front garden. There was enough light to spend a satisfying hour in the garden before dark. Bent over a flowerbed, I heard the most unusual hissing click, finished off with a small cough. I looked around carefully. I was a little anxious, being absolutely alone, with not even a dog for company. Seeing nothing, I continued weeding.

This curious noise was resumed energetically. I walked to the corner of the house, looked round it, then went down towards the vineyards. There was nothing. I was about to start weeding again when a barrage of sound hit me, coming from above. I looked up in the tree under which I was weeding, into the great golden eyes of a large owl. Seeing that she had my attention, she lifted her wings away from her body and uttered several clicks.

I stood upright, lifted my elbows away from my body and clicked back at her. She seemed astonished. Myself, I thought it only polite, if this was Owl for introductions.

The second time there was a variation: hiss, click, hiss, click. She waited. I returned her message. She cocked her head at me, then flew in a wide circle down to the vines and back again.

'Show off,' I said. 'I can't do that, and you know it. However, if you are fussed that I want to sit in your tree, don't bother. I have other things to occupy myself.' This news was received with several slower clicks.

Then she did a curious thing. She flew out of the tree and onto the ground. Walking very slowly, stopping every metre or so to look at me, she crossed the lawn and hopped into another oak tree. It happened to be in a direct line with my bedroom window, just off the edge of an open veranda.

Well, I didn't understand this kind of behaviour at all. It must have had some significance for her, but not for me. I finished the weeding. It was twilight, and I decided my stomach was more important at that moment, so I went into the house to make supper.

The next morning was Sunday, all day. Oh, what heaven! I snuggled into the sheets and turned on the radio to savour the early morning concert. I was lost in Grieg when a torrent of hisses and clicks erupted out of the tree from Mrs Owl. I got up to have a look. The tree into which she had climbed the previous evening was directly in my line of vision. Two tiny owls were being shoved out of a hollow in the great tree trunk onto a broad, flat lateral branch. The logistical problem was being caused by the first little owl, the larger of the two. He would not shift up the branch to make space for his brother. He was resolute: 'Not moving, Ma, not another inch.' The smaller brother had one leg on the branch and one in the hollow, so was doing a fair imitation of the splits and not finding it comfortable, and was weakly squeaking out his displeasure.

Since I found out many years ago that someone in my immediate family was anti-Semitic, I have always given my pets Jewish names. The little owls became Benjamin and Samuel instantly. I looked at them. They both had what appeared to be a crew cut. The tiny vertical feathers above their ears and across their brows gave them an expression of astonishment. Their eyes were very round. The rest of their tiny bodies was covered in a mottled grey down.

Mrs Owl, with some great effort, managed to shove Benjamin further along the branch so that his little brother was finally accommodated. She sat so close to Samuel, he was almost smothered. Benjamin, who by now had got the hang of sitting upright on the branch, had moved along away from his mother. Mrs Owl leapt to the other side of him and shuffled him back again, wing to wing against Samuel. That seemed the entertainment for the morning, so I went back to the music.

At this juncture I feel it's appropriate to tell you about my mother. She was unquestionably a Dr Dolittle incarnate. She spoke Cow, Dog, Mossie, Bulbul, Praying Mantis, Mole, Mouse, Chicken and Rooster, Chameleon, Owl, Hadeda, Frog and Sheep, among other animal languages. She stopped short of Snake and Spider. In fact, she was a terrible embarrassment to me. She would start conversations with animals as we walked the dusty farm roads to take the only bus of the day into town. She had once leapt over our fence to separate two Jersey bulls belonging to the farmer next door, who were vying for the favours of a heifer just come into season. They did actually stop butting each other, and she stood between them, lecturing them on the proper rites of courtship, which as far as she was concerned did not include bovine gangbangs.

The Rand Agricultural Show was held near Wits University every Easter. We spent hours looking at the cattle, and, as we walked along, untethered animals simply followed her. It was comical to see the owners running after her, trying to restrain their animals, but, worse, it was difficult trying to get into an exhibition hall with three cows and a bull fighting for entry too.

She loved poultry. They loved her. After a few words from mother, along the lines of 'Oh, you gorgeous boy, aren't you the most beautiful handsome coucou I have ever seen?' (this said in a crooning voice, dripping with honey, to a rooster standing forlorn in his cage), the rooster would immediately lift his head, fluff up his feathers, crow and scratch the straw. In retrospective, for I was too young then to think of such matters, speaking to one's loved one along these lines each day might ensure more cordial marital relations.

At mother's words, the collective poultry would put on mating displays, dragging their wings along the ground, do little dances, crow unceasingly, lay eggs, and fight each other besides. One could follow her progress by the raucous noise which ensued from the lines of cages around the hall. Talking to an owl was very small potatoes as far as my family were concerned.

We had started the picking season. It was the end of November. Oh, the darling little Methley plums, to be on the table for the British on Christmas Day. The following two weeks seemed to leave no room to stare at owls, and they were all very quiet. Bill, Daddy, my sister Yvonne and my niece arrived for holidays. I was in the pack-shed most of the day, and it was wonderful to eat beautiful meals cooked by Yvonne.

My father, at eighty, was the one who could 'stand and stare'.

He reported the daily goings-on of the owl family. One early Sunday morning, again lying late in bed, I heard a tremendous ruckus from Mrs Owl. She was screeching, clicking and hissing up a storm. I went to open the shutters. The window was open and there, not a hand's length away, was Benjamin. Clearly he had decided to test his flight potential and had landed on a table right under the bedroom window. We had placed it there because the other side of the veranda was unshaded and hot in the afternoon. It was convenient to have supper there and watch the sunset. Perhaps he mistook it for another branch.

Benjamin was very close to me. It was so hot that I hadn't worn a nightgown. He was definitely horrified at being confronted by the vast expanse of pink person. I bent down to have a better look at him. He was adorable. He didn't think the same about me, and was backing away from this apparition as fast as possible. Not having a rear-view mirror, he fell onto the floor, then gathering himself, raced to the end of the veranda, clambered up the edging flower box, and yelled for his mother.

Mrs Owl was hysterical. 'Benjamin,' I was sure she was saying, 'don't I tell you, stay home with Momma. Why do you have to go exploring? Isn't this tree enough for you? I have made a nice home here. Children, really, what do they want?'

Benjamin was unforthcoming on the subject. With a test flap or two of his tiny wings, rather reminiscent of the Wright brothers in early flight, he launched himself into space. Clinging and then crawling up the stem of the tree, he arrived on the home branch. Mrs Owl groomed him, and fussed and scolded him. I know that feeling – I had an adventurous eldest son myself.

Days passed in a blur of activity, all concentrated on plums and the first peaches. Off the tree, into sacks, into bins, drive the tractor to the pack-shed. Eat, sleep, and start again the next day, and not much else.

Another morning, very early, saw a different Owl family crisis. I opened the shutters to watch it. A large squirrel had incautiously decided to reclaim his home of the previous season. Mrs Owl took exception, and she flew at him with beak and claw. Squirrel lost the plot completely. Instead of retreating directly down the tree, he simply rushed round and round the trunk, but he didn't get any closer to the ground.

This enraged Mother Owl. She decided to dive-bomb him. The problem with this line of attack was that she had to push herself off the tree, get levitation, and then aim for the squirrel. By the time all these flight plans were operative, Squirrel was round the other side of the tree, literally behind her. It was a riot. I was whooping encouragement, unfairly, for the squirrel, to keep the farce going. But then sanity kicked in, and he fled down the trunk of the tree to quieter accommodation.

❖

It was Christmas Eve. The pack-shed had closed at 4 p.m. the previous day. There was to be peace and quiet for four days. Bill rushed into the bedroom. 'Gwen, Benjamin is on the ground and can't get up the tree,' he said.

'Oh, don't be silly, of course he can get up the tree.' I was not going to pander to this nonsense.

An hour later I went outside, and there was this bundle of belligerent baby feathers still standing on the ground. I sat down on the lawn. I was no more than a foot away from him. 'Now look here, Benjamin, you are too young to be a delinquent. You know how extravagantly your mother behaves. Don't spoil her Christmas. Just turn around and crawl up to your house. We are having a nice brunch later on, and you had better be on your branch, at home.'

Hiss, hiss. Click, click, hiss! from Benjamin. I hissed and clicked back. He was twenty centimetres high, for goodness' sake, and full of opinions. Benjamin carried on with another flurry of clicks, then, turning his back on me, he walked round the oak tree. Just another adolescent having the last word! He could find his own damn way home.

I went into the kitchen to help Yvonne with her preparations, which were well under way. There was a tortilla filled with potatoes, fresh thyme and onions. Grilled tomatoes, grilled red and yellow peppers, with capers and anchovies, bathed in olive oil. Tapenade, the peanut butter of Provence, to spread on the walnut bread called 'fougasse'. An exquisite platter of sliced summer fruit. Blueberry muffins warm from the oven. Champagne and coffee. And best of all, the thought that there was no picking, packing, arguing, shouting, for four whole days. Oh, what perfect bliss!

Enter from left, my partner in a state of high agitation. 'Gwen, Benjamin is lost.'

'How do you know?' I asked.

'Well, I could swear his mother is crying. She looks suicidal,' he says.

This comment, coming from an accountant? No, no, this is how my mother used to speak.

Heaven help us, all eccentricity is contagious. I go out to the front garden and look at the family branch, leaving Yvonne with the preparations. Mrs Owl looks distraught. Head and wings hanging, she is sitting next to Samuel, looking at the ground, beak slightly open, in utter misery.

Well, all we could do was go and look for the little wretch. We spread out, peered into flowerbeds, under shrubs, down paths. No Benjamin. Daddy and I decided to try the peach orchard – after all, if your legs are just upwards of six centimetres long you can't go far. But he had gone far, relatively speaking. About fifty metres away, under the peach trees, there he was examining a fallen peach. He turned his head to look at us. 'It rolls, Mom, look!' He continued clicking, clearly pleased with his new toy.

Enough was enough. Daddy fetched a fruit box and a tray while I kept guard. Maybe owls have rejection responses, I thought, so I didn't want to touch the little bird. I put the box smartly over his head and slid the tray under the box. He would have no option but to climb onto the tray, and *voila!*, he was transportable. I lifted up the tray, box on top, and there was no little owl on the ground. Round one to us! We walked back up to the house.

Calling Bill, I asked him to fetch a long ladder. With that in place, Bill climbed up into the tree hollow. He took the tray from me and popped Benjamin into the front door.

Mrs Owl had been sulking high above on another branch. The sudden reappearance of her elder son was too much for her. She launched into a tirade of recrimination. 'Benjamin, my boy, why do you do this? You keep leaving home. Don't I bring you food? You got a mouse for supper this evening! My best, is it not good enough? Benjamin, you are breaking Momma's heart.' Well, it sounded like something along those lines. The clicking, inter-spersed with screeches and hissing, went on and on. Benjamin's view was that it was Momma having a tantrum, just because he wanted to explore. He shrugged his little shoulders, and stared out at the mountains.

During all this, Yvonne had been busy. She had set the table with a pretty pink linen tablecloth, a posy of flowers, silver and napkins. Wonderful plates made by our inspired local potter Valerie were all set in place. Then Yvonne brought out our feast. It looked scrumptious!

We had just pulled out the chairs and sat down when Mrs Owl ruffled her feathers, called out several times in a husky cry, and evidently decided that a grand gesture was in order.

I could not later work out if it was gratitude for the return of Benjamin or fury at the intrusion just when she was settling down to a quiet life with Sam. Mrs Owl flew out of the tree in a tight circle. On returning, she flew just above our heads, emptying her bowels over the lunch as she went. An unidentifiable piece of insect ended up against the tortilla. A partially digested mouse leg had missed the muffins by a millimetre. Various bits of 'God knows what', to quote my shell-shocked niece, had landed on the butter, in a wine glass, and on a tomato.

It was impossible to be upset. We collapsed laughing. We

cleared the table, changed the linen, and rescued what we could. Mrs Owl was nuzzling her firstborn and crooning with happiness. We had a wonderful feast, toasting Mrs Owl and her babies for giving us hours of interest and amusement. We bubbled along with the champagne, and stored away a memory to keep forever.

9

Japie's Story

I arrive at Japie and Maria's house. A small determined dog is bark-ing loudly and looking aggressive. Maria comes to let me in. I ask about the small dog. 'Nay, Miz Gwen, hy is net 'n speeldingetjie.' I settle down to hear Japie's story.

❖

I was born in Ceres. I was the *laatlammetjie* of the family. Number nine of the children, and six years after the last one. It was 1927, on 6 September. The farm on which my parents lived was called Rooikamp. It was the colour of the earth, red and rich. It was a mixed farm of sheep and cattle and crop food. It was very big. The lands ran across many hills.

When I was eight years old we moved to Calvinia. That was

mostly sheep-farming, and when I was very small I went out with my father. Then I had sheep to look after by myself. Also, in the lambing season I could help because I had small hands and could get the lambs' feet out if they were stuck inside the mother before they were born.

I also had to tie up the donkeys for all the ploughs in the morning, and I tell you that in winter, when the ice was on the ground, the tethers were so stiff and cold I was crying to get it done before the farmer punished me.

My mother was very unhappy there and after three years we moved back to Ceres. I had a proper job then and we had a sort of school, so I got my letters and could read a bit. Then we moved again. Some of the older children were working on other farms.

My father took us to the Koue Bokkeveld. You know, Miz Gwen, you can get into the Karoo in three ways. We went in by Worcester. I worked then with my father, but I was getting older, and so I went and found my own job in Wolseley. I worked there for a little while, but then my mother had moved to Franschhoek. She came from a Franschhoek family.

She had found a job in the kitchen, and also sorting all the raisins, on one of the farms. A lot of the farms were doing that. They turned their grapes into raisins, because the wine was not selling. KWV didn't pay good prices. This was 1943, so they could not export to England because of the War. When all the grapes were sorted and dried to make the raisins, then they would be taken by bakkie to Wellington for packing and so on.

There were also a lot of sheep in Franschhoek, and I thought I could look after them, because I had done that already. Also, Miz Gwen, I loved my mother and I missed her. I longed for her touch and for Franschhoek.

I stayed on the farm Grootgewag. The farm was owned by a German named Heyndrich. He had one leg a little bit shorter than the other. He used to lean over to one side every time he landed on the shorter leg. We called him Trap-in-die-Gaatjie. Now the farm is owned by Mr and Mrs Parkfelt.

I collected the hens' eggs every day. Hulle was wild, en die boggers they bit me and pecked me so much, my hands were bleeding sore. The hens laid their eggs all over the farm, so I collected them in a basket and took them to the kitchen, then washed them in the sink.

There, one day, I saw this young girl. Her name was Maria. She was twelve years old. She did not look at me for three days. Then, one evening, she looked right at me, and gave me her eyes. I knew I had found my girl. From that day, the whole world was different. I saw her every day in the kitchen, when I brought in the eggs. We did not speak for another week, but then I asked her to walk with me to the river. We walked out when the sun was down, there was a little warm wind, just enough to move the folds of her skirt, and she did not speak, but we touched each other.

Next to the river I kissed her, and the inside of her mouth was smoother than an eggshell, but warmer and softer, and so I began to teach her about love. From then, I have never wanted anyone else. Two years after that, we got married. After we were married for some time, we went back to Rawsonville to work for Tommy de Wit. It was a grape farm, and also there a lot of the grapes were dried for raisins, but most of it went to the cellars. It was for sweet wine, it was almost all hanepoot.

It was a very bitter eight years, we had a very hard time with that man. The hours of work were winter and summer 6 a.m. to 6 p.m. There was half an hour for breakfast and half an hour for lunch. Saturday and Sunday you had to work from 6 to 8 a.m. for no money, because he said that was for your sick pay. If you got sick you didn't get your money, you lost your money. If you left and you had never been sick, you got nothing.

On Saturday we got paid after eight o'clock, then we were told to get on the back of the lorry and we went to the village to buy our food. If the women annoyed the farmer, he kicked them or hit them. If he got cross with the men, he hit them with a leather strap.

I could not stand to watch my wife suffering. She was not from here. We were both so tired. We decided to go back to Franschhoek. We got work on Keerweder, and stayed for 22 years. It was a fruit and vegetable farm, and some cattle, and they also made vinegar to sell.

❖

The *speeldingetjie* dog leaps to his short legs and starts yapping – but it is Japie's sons coming back home after collecting wives and girlfriends from shopping. They ask who I am and what I am doing. Japie and Maria launch into a full-scale description of my storycollecting, and Japie says, 'En ons is in die boek, en dit gaan in die winkels wees,' and Benjamin, his baby son, says, 'Nee, Pa, ek glo nie.' I interrupt and tell Benjamin what a good storyteller his father is, and Japie says, 'Lees vir hulle, Miz Gwen,' and so I do. The room falls silent, and they learn for the first time of their father's life. He had not spoken of it to them before.

10

The Story from Krige Siebrits

Pieter Siebrits came to Franschhoek in 1946 and bought 150 morgen of land for eight thousand English pounds. The Rawbone family owned it at the time.

The Mantell family was living on La Terra de Luc, and the Maskies on the hill at Swiss Farm, which they had built. The Keslers, and Ettie and Simon Berkowitsz, who owned the Central Hotel, had been there from the early thirties. It is said that General Smuts so loved Ettie's Jewish cooking that, whenever he could, he had a Sunday lunch there. The Michelsons arrived in 1942. This was the entire English contingent at the time.

Pieter's ancestor Franz Siebrits had arrived at the Cape in 1774, from Germany. The farm, called Keerweder because it was as far as one could go into the Valley, was originally given to a German in appreciation for his spying activities for the Dutch East India Company. The Dutch were a suspicious lot, and with the language and political problems in the country they needed informers. The French Huguenots at the Cape were a threat because they continued to speak French, and they refused to give up their religion and become Dutch Reformed adherents. To them, it may have felt like the persecution by the Catholics all over again.

Krige Siebrits was Pieter's son, one of six brothers. He was born in his Ouma's house, Groenelande, on Main Road, Paarl. His Oupa already had the farm Cabrière. Franschhoek was a small village at the time, and remote. There were only a few visitors and they usually knew people or were family. The tar road stopped at the upper end of the village, and the Huguenot Monument had not yet been built.

In 1920 Keerweder became the first guest house in Franschhoek. Guests from Cape Town were fetched by horse cart from Klapmuts station. The guests were accommodated in the family bedrooms and some outbuildings converted for the purpose. They ate with the family and had a real glimpse of farm life.

One young couple visiting the farm got engaged during a romantic weekend. The young man produced a diamond ring, and, before slipping it onto his future bride's finger, scratched the date and their initials onto a pane of glass in the house. Recently the grandchildren of the couple asked permission to visit the farm, to see the window where the pane is marked.

Krige grew up in Franschhoek and went to the Franschhoek school up to matric. He then began working for his father. His duties were everything and anything: being in the vineyards, learning to prune, thin fruit, pick, pack, clear, plough, spray. His pay was half a crown a day, or two shillings and sixpence – probably worth about ten rands today. He got Saturday afternoon and Sunday off. Later, when he was much more useful, his father gave him ten pounds per month.

There was a general dealer where Spar is today. It held groceries, wool, fabrics, cotton and sheen, bicycles, tools, ammunition, hides, drinks, medicines, lamps, batteries, clothing, fruit, dress patterns, schoolbooks, uniforms, tools, pens, paper, seeds and sweets, which were a luxury. They were stored in huge glass jars on the counter, with a screw-on lid. Nigger balls were two for a penny, and all the marzipan sweets were three for a penny.

On Thursday Krige's father placed the order for the week. On Friday, at eleven in the morning, everything was delivered to the farm by horse cart. One paid the total bill at the end of the month. The farmers always paid in cash.

The delivery horses were stabled across the road at Oudestallen in big wooden stables. The horses had a very nice life there, and lots of people used to buy them carrots and lumps of sugar. They were lavishly spoilt by all the customers and passers-by.

In the spring a young man's fancy lightly turns to thoughts of love. Krige met his wife Christine in the village. She had come from Citrusdal, north-west of Franschhoek. She was slender, with grey-green eyes, and there was a way she looked at him that made him blush and have yearnings which he could not describe.

There were very few work opportunities in the Boland for a girl. You were never offered the family farm – it always went to the eldest son. You could be a nurse, a teacher, or work at the Co-op or other shops – the post office, Standard Bank, the station (as a clerk), or the municipality. Christine was working at the Co-op and earned forty rands per month. A garage in Malmesbury offered her sixty. She had to make the decision over the weekend.

Krige's father stepped into the breach. 'No, I have made a decision. She is not going to take that job,' he announced while carving the Sunday leg of lamb, the large family seated around him and Christine in their midst. 'It is much, much cheaper for my son to do his *vrying* here in Franschhoek than to drive to Malmesbury three times a week.' He turned to Christine. 'I will pay you the extra twenty rands a month to stay here.'

She accepted the offer, and some time afterwards another offer, of marriage. They settled into a cottage on the farm, and into married life, with children being part of the plan. 'I still love her and like her as much as I did then, Gwen. She is a wonderful devoted and loving woman. We courted for four years before marrying, but I made sure we were right for one another and so did she.'

Krige carefully observed the trains going by. The train service to Paarl began in 1905. There were eight sidings along the route. Opposite Le Bonheur came the siding named Celliers, then Simondium, Groot Drakenstein, Lategan siding at Bellingham, Wemmershoek, La Motte, La Provence, and finally Franschhoek station. In the beginning the train service was one train in the morning and one in the evening. The train 'slept' in Franschhoek.

Going to Paarl, you went by train. From Celliers siding to Paarl cost fourpence. All the schoolchildren used the trains, and no one had anything to fear. The smallest children used to travel alone. Afterwards there were two services to Paarl per day.

During harvest time the train was loaded at various sidings until 4 p.m., then it went back to Paarl. If you missed it at one siding you could go in your bakkie to the next one and still get things onto the train. If you were riding along the road and there was a crossing, you could wave your hat like mad and just load up right there. It helped if you gave the driver a couple of cigarettes or a packet of raisins, or maybe a bottle of wine.

One of the important services to the community was the delivery of guano to the farmers. It was collected off the West Coast islands of Dassen, Malgas, Vondeling and Jutten, all near Langebaan. Boats would come over with prisoners, who scraped it off the rocks and beaches, then it was put in big bags, loaded on the train and delivered to the closest rail point. In this case, it was offloaded at all the sidings. It was called government guano. The farmers said it was *peperduur*, as it cost eight pounds a ton and the railage was two shillings for the fifty miles from Langebaan.

Farm manure from cattle, and sheep manure, were available for two to three pounds for an 'ES bogie'. This name was for two open railway trucks joined together. Compared to the guano, it was a bargain, but every second year the farmers had to use the other to nourish the soil.

The caretaker on the islands used to collect penguin eggs, and they were sold all over South Africa. Some were also exported to England. Other eggs also went travelling, in a sense. Tante Lottie Hugo had a farm opposite Groendal called Dennegeur. One morning when she was walking down the garden she noticed that the train stopped at the siding, the stoker got out, and in a few minutes the train left again. Quite by chance she was in the garden the next day and the same thing happened. She was busy for a day or two, and then she watched carefully. The train stopped, the stoker got out, and then after two minutes left again.

Now, being a modest lady, she thought that it was peculiar that the stoker's need to empty his bladder occurred at exactly the same time each day, but what else could he be doing?

She went down to the siding to look around. She happened to have turkeys that laid eggs all over the farm. One of the more regular nests was just below the railway line in a clump of bushes. The nest was empty. Well, come to think of it, it had been empty for quite a while, and yet the same turkeys were grazing close by. 'Jirre, ek weet,' she thought, having a sudden idea. 'Daai bogger steel my eiers!'

She was a lady of some resource. She fetched a turkey egg from the pantry and wrote on it. Her message said, 'Waar is my ander eiers?' The next day she watched carefully as the train stopped and out climbed the stoker. He went to the nest, picked up the egg, and quickly put it back. The train never stopped there again except by request, and Tante Lottie was able to breed a lot more turkeys.

At that time Wiggen's Store was near the present antique shop in Main Road. Then it became Swannie's Shop, owned by Neil le Roux's maternal Oupa after he came back from Klerksdorp. The present First National Bank site was a blacksmith's. The smith fixed wagon bands, shod horses, made kitchen items, and could fix anything made of metal.

One day a farmer came in with a bent ploughshare. He asked if it could be fixed. 'Natuurlik,' said the blacksmith. He heated the metal over the roaring fire for a while, held it in a huge pair of pliers, and with one well-aimed whack of his hammer it was straightened. The farmer asked how much it cost. 'Vyf shillings,' said the blacksmith.

'Vyf shillings!' yelled the farmer. 'How dare you overcharge me. I want a detailed invoice now.' The farmer was enraged.

He received the invoice, which read:

1 hou met die hamer	1/-
Weet waar om te slaan	4/-
Totaal	5/-

The farmer paid.

11

Peetie

A black man came to Franschhoek in 1952, Krige said. His name was Petrus Maponda. He was eighteen years old, and from Tanganyika by way of the coalfield in Natal.

Japie heard the story from Peetie. Strong men had come to his village when Peetie was fifteen and ordered the younger men and boys to get on the back of a lorry. They were sjambokked if they asked questions. When they were on the trucks, they were told they were going to get work just up the road. Two weeks later they arrived in Dundee, Natal.

The work was arranged by the foreign minister of Tanganyika, who 'sold' young black men to the South African coal industry. They had to send half their wages back home and it was chopped from their pay, but their families never got the money.

Peetie told me he worked in Dundee for eight months. He hated the dark and the dust of the tunnels with a ferocious hatred. The heat and the small spaces, the closeness of working body to body with men, made him almost deranged.

Peetie was a child of the vast golden savannahs of East Africa. The light and space of the high plateaus had shaped him, as had the effervescent air of high altitudes. To work like a rat in the dark was unendurable. 'Working there, Miz Gwen,' he told me, 'was like you have died and gone to hell. I had to take breath, or I could not live.' He dropped his head when he said this. There are stored memories that have the ability through time, however long, to make us weep. I reached out my hand, and he took it, in his gentle way, with both of his.

One day in Natal he took up his possessions, meagre as they were, and walked towards the Cape. He worked along the way, and walked down the coast. 'Oh, Miz Gwen, when I saw the sea, and the smell of the air, I was so happy I was dancing. I did know I was in a good place.' He got to Cape Town in 1952. The journey had taken him two years.

He spent six months in Cape Town but yearned for the country. That's why he went to Franschhoek. Japie remembers Peetie's life and fortunes there. Peetie asked for a job on Keerweder and was put in charge of the milking and caring for the cows. He had been herding cows since he was four years old, and so he became the dairy manager. From the first day, the cows would follow his softly spoken instructions, and became attached to him with almost dog-like devotion.

After a few months in the Valley, Peetie did what everyone else was doing, and he started to drink wine. This was much better than the stuff he had to drink up North, and better than *tshwala*, the 'kaffir beer' on the mines. Life was *akuna matatu* – in Swahili, 'no problem' – because he had found a community and a special girl to call his own. The cows loved him, with his small gentle hands, and no one else could get the same amount of milk from them. He would croon to them in Swahili, milking all the while, telling them stories of golden lions, giraffes and elephants, of birds who came to ride on the winds which brought black clouds to the great plains and the Rift Valley.

Unfortunately, one Friday afternoon Peetie anticipated the weekend rather early in the day. By milking time he was unable to sit on the milking stool and continually fell off, sometimes rolling under the cow. Liefling, the best milk producer, had to give him a shove with her foot to get him to stand up, which he tried to do, right under her. A kick got him upright, but not for long. He was also singing loud songs of battles and conquest, and told stories to the cows of running off with seventeen human heifers, all for himself. The cows thought this was quite normal. Didn't the bull that came around every season do the same thing? They went on chewing the cud, hoping he would come to his senses and relieve them of the milk stretching their udders.

He didn't. He was in a deep alcoholic daze lying on top of Liefling's food in the manger, and wouldn't move even when she licked him. Krige went into the stable to see what was happening, as Peetie had not come to the kitchen with the milk at the usual time. He found Peetie lying oblivious in the manger, snoring loudly. Peetie woke up in the police cells, and Krige went back to the stables to milk the cows. After getting a pitiful amount of milk from the first two cows, he had to admit defeat. The cows were not used to his hands, which were bigger and stronger, and pulled on them. They didn't like the change and, besides, this human being never told them stories. Like a group of prissy women, they simply withheld their favours.

Krige went back to the police station and asked them to let Peetie out to do the milking, and then lock him up again. The whole weekend was spent in this troublesome way, Peetie milking streams of milk into the bucket, reminding Krige each day how much he needed him. For Krige it was a hollow victory.

Krige's Ma had two dogs, a small yappy dog and another, a serious dog, big and unfriendly. The little dog used to bark at Peetie when he came into the kitchen with the milk. On this day the little dog was in a frenzy of barking, and the big dog crossed the room quietly and bit Peetie in the leg. Peetie leapt over to the little dog and hit him hard. Krige asked him why. 'Nee, master, it is the little dog that tells him to bite me. I must hit the small dog, not the big one,' said Peetie, nursing his leg.

Another weekend proved rather more disastrous. Peetie had been put on pills to stop him drinking. The cure was to make him violently ill if he mixed wine with the pills. This was intended to make him give up wine. No one thought of other forms of alcohol. Krige's Ouma had a huge bottle of '4711' eau de cologne on her dressing table in front of the bedroom window. Peetie slid a hand through the window, had a good slug of the toilette water, and was immediately happily drunk on almost pure alcohol, smelling most delectable at the same time. This *dop* became a habit, and was discovered when Ouma, who was tarting up for a social occasion, found the bottle nearly empty. Peetie began buying his own supply of cologne. The chemist remarked that he must be *vrying* a lot of women, to need all this cologne.

Peetie could now indulge whenever the need arose, and he was once more in the stables sleeping in the manger. Krige was so angry he tied him to the manger and left him there for the night, lying in the straw. This was an enormous insult to Peetie. He was furious, packed his things, and left the farm from that September until April the next year. Then he returned one day, with his small suitcase, and said to Krige, 'Ek wil huistoe kom.' He stayed for the next 48 years until his death in 2002.

When Krige's father died, Peetie sat with Krige through his grief, and said, 'Die ou toppie is nou nie hier nie, nou is jy my Pa. Ek sal jou nooit verlaat.' And he never did, until he was taken to his burial ground.

'I loved that little man, Gwen,' Krige told me. 'He was the most trustworthy, obliging, honest, helpful and cheerful human being I have ever met. I miss him just like one of my brothers.' I knew what he was talking about – I loved Peetie too. There was something about Peetie that one couldn't define. He was a dear and valued person in my life.

12

Making Jam

Once I had got the hang of judging the size, shape and colour of every little plum that would fulfil the requirements of the pack-shed, I was appalled at the amount of reject fruit that did not meet the standard. I wanted to do my best in this new venture, so keeping up the quality of the fruit delivered to the pack-shed was a priority. Each day there were crates and crates of fruit that weren't acceptable – the plums that were scorched by a wire, a small hail nick, a shape not quite right, a bird peck or something, which would disqualify it from being saleable.

Having grown up on a farm where nothing went to waste, my sister and I had been initiated at an early age into making jam and preserving all manner of things. I had made jam all my life, and decided to make jam out of the Methley rejects. The Methley is a small plum, ripe at the end of November, which cooks beautifully. The jam cooks into a glowing wine colour.

I was not going to use pickers or packers, as they were too fully occupied. A quick word of mouth produced a few nursing mothers, several Oumas, and one or two visiting Aunties who could come up to the house for some hours a day. I bought a tin bath and eight small sharp knives. Seating was arranged on the back veranda, and the ladies sat on cushions on top of overturned fruit cases. Jam-making was started.

In the afternoons I weighed the fruit and sugar, left it overnight, then in the morning it took an hour to be boiled, skimmed and bottled. I bought six dozen bottles. While I was running around the farm and pack-shed, Daddy – in residence at the time – was in charge of the stirring and skimming. During the boiling, the white sugary foam rose to the top. If it was not skimmed off quickly, it would cover the stove in sticky goo and cloud the jam. It was put into bowls and, once cooled, given to the many children to lick off spoons.

The ladies arrived and, as everything was set up on the back veranda, they started working immediately. I had appointed a tea lady, who kept the others well supplied. Packets of muffin mix could be whipped up and baked for those in need of sustenance. I showed them how to cut the fruit and take out any blemishes. They worked wonderfully well, and with friends around them the time passed quickly. Settled comfortably, they could talk to their hearts' content and earn some money while doing so.

An hour later I went to see the progress and was astonished. Half the bath was full of prepared fruit. I checked out the four jam kettles I had inherited from my mother. Although very large, they were hopelessly inadequate for the quantities of fruit we had. I went to Paarl and bought another three. More *uitval* was being brought out of the pack-shed. At the end of the day I had to tell the ladies to take a day off, as I needed a gap to deal with the sheer quantity of fruit processed.

At lunchtime I went down to the village to buy another fifty pounds of sugar and twelve dozen bottles. The evening was spent weighing fruit and sugar into various pots. In the morning the fruit and sugar had amalgamated. It went on to the stove immediately and was cooked within twenty minutes once it got to the boil, but it had to be stirred almost non-stop. Since I was getting up at 5.30 a.m., I turned the stove on and had the jam boiling by 6. The first day everything went like clockwork.

Unnoticed by me, Daddy had put the bowls of scalding sugar foam out to cool on a high garden wall closing off the back yard. The sweet sugary messages were carried to the far corners of the Valley and beyond by a light breeze. Those with the right olfactory receptors inhaled this delicious whiff of sugar and started sending bee-radar invitations to every corner of the Boland: 'Attention! *Achtung! Attenzione!* There is a Bee Happening! Come Fly with Me! Entrance Free. Nectar, rivers of nectar for *free*.'

The messages were picked up during the next day. Bee families decided to put forward their annual holiday. Questions were asked around the family hive. Shall we take the children? We take the children but I am not taking your mother. They set their direction finders and booked into Patrysfontein, up on the Pass Road. Their journeys began.

The next day we reviewed our strategy and decided that if we were going to do this seriously, it should be on more efficient lines. More ladies were recruited. There were now two circles of women cutting fruit, and two cycles of cooking. Bottling was done late at night. Where was I going to sell it? I went down to Pippin Farm Stall and asked Hendy if he would be interested. 'Yes, OK, but bring me some to taste.' I did. 'Well, it's not as sweet as usual, but I'll take a dozen bottles,' says Hendy.

It was on the third day of making jam that it happened. My father, aged 80 but still tactful, arrived in the pack-shed. He coughed. 'Uhmm, Gwen, uhmm, I think you'd better come into the house.'

'Why, Daddy? I am hellish busy at the moment,' I said, not really paying attention.

'Well, uhmm, I think you should come,' he said again. Since my father was the most self-effacing and diffident man, I followed him outside.

'Don't go through the kitchen. You can't,' he said, taking my hand and leading me round the front of the house. When I got to the kitchen I found all the women crowded in there too.

'What is going on?' I asked.

'Come and look, merrim, but don't open a window or a door.' They all appeared to be in a state of shock.

I pushed through the women and went to the window. Three full swarms of bees had taken up residence in the enclosed yard. On the outside edges of the swarms were the worker bees, all frantically active. Thousands of bees were clustered along the top third of the wall. All the rows of soup plates, saucers and bowls of 'skim' from the jam that Father had put on top of the wall had disappeared. The only thing one could see was hundreds if not thousands of bees. Perhaps a hundred wasps had also arrived, and they shot through the air like fighter jets, trying to penetrate the mass of bees clustered over the long line of bowls, which were invisible.

Bees in their tens of thousands covered all the walls. A huge plane tree was a seething mass of bees. One could hardly see that it had leaves – there were layers of bees on every single surface, even on the ground. The air was thick with them, and their buzzing was a subdued roar. The dogs were hiding under the kitchen table. Two had been stung and were whimpering, so we administered lemon juice to the stings. The other two knew something was out of order, and were alert and growling softly.

'Well, first of all, get all the children inside, and close the pack-shed doors. Tell everyone to come in here.' Two ladies went off to give the warnings. In a few minutes we were all crowded into the kitchen and dining-room. The ladies thought we should have a little something for our nerves, so they put the kettle on, and the cups were brought out. I closed my eyes to bottles being opened.

I asked how it had all happened. 'Sien jy, merrim' – they were just coming back after lunch. They noticed one swarm of bees going up to settle in the blue-gum trees along the Pass Road above our dam. They remarked on it to each other. Then they saw another swarm of bees coming through the air like a rolled-up blanket, they were so closely packed, and they landed somewhat closer to the house. The ladies walked a bit more quickly towards the house, where they found one swarm already in residence in the yard. They had to walk round to the front door to get in, and decided not to go outside under any circumstances.

'Then we sent Oupa to go and get you, Miz Gwen,' they said.

I phoned Diffie at the police station. The sergeant in charge, he was one of my son Pete's drinking friends. Well, he didn't really know what to suggest. He couldn't arrest them or charge them with loitering.

'Any chance on crowd control, or malicious intent to dogs?' I asked.

'Gwen, I have got better things to do than make jokes. Goodbye.'

Eureka! The bottlers of the famous, meltingly delicious Champagne Honey also live in Franschhoek. Andrew, a scion of the family and used to bees, was another of Pete's friends. I phoned Andrew and explained the situation. Well, he couldn't come up now, but when the sun went down he would have a look. Bees got quieter then. 'Send the jam makers home.' Nonsense! The jam makers were set up in the dining-room around the table. The afternoon passed. The pickers went about their business in the orchards in perfect safety, as every single bee or wasp was in the yard. Finally everyone left, and the sun sank lower, behind the ridge of hills.

The evenings in Franschhoek are compellingly seductive. All one's senses are activated. There are a number of elements which conspire to make it thus. Most men work at home. There is a sense of involvement by all members of the families, and by everyone, in

78

the activities of the day. Once work is over, there are no traffic jams to face, just the tranquillity of the landscape, and the long twilight hours. Moments before sunset, a south wind comes whispering over the hills, and the temperature drops a few degrees. There's the prospect of a good dinner, eaten while watching the sun slide behind the hills, under the rose-gold sky. It is magical. Then there is the pleasure of the twilight air, which smells of vanilla, dust and honey. Holding the first cooled glass of white wine in one's hand, and music playing – heaven for the soul.

I checked out the yard. Yes, the buzzing was quietening down. There were not as many bees along the top of the wall. The rims of the dishes could be seen in the dusk, pale circles of white porcelain, like upturned eyes under water. Even the outlines of the plane trees were visible. Of course! The bees had imbibed all the fruit nectar. As soon as it was finished there would be no reason to stay, as we had nothing else in blossom or bloom at the time.

Andrew arrived promptly. We sat companionably in the dusk, each drinking a glass of wine. When he judged the bees were quiet he went to look. I followed. He took out his torch, shone it around, and began to laugh. 'What is so funny?' I asked. He explained. Because of the seasonal nature of blossoms of whatever kind, bees spend a lot of energy flying back and forth to their hive to deposit their nectar. Whatever they feast on is what keeps them going. In this case it was like having a bar opened beside a take-away, with a three-star restaurant attached.

The fruit nectar issued appealing invitations. 'Drink your fill and don't move, eat as much as you can. Home is just four metres away.' The bees responded willingly, rapturously!

They were now in the grip of a sugar fix, far worse than alcoholics. In the beam we could see bees leaning against each other. Single bees couldn't quite work out where it was they wanted to go. They tried to fly, failed, then simply crawled over other bee bodies in search of some random destination they had in mind. Many were lying on their backs kicking their legs feebly. Others, directionless, were droning around in circles. All of them were without the frantic energy of the early afternoon.

Overdosed on sugar, the lot of them. It was funny. I joined him, laughing. 'Doesn't this remind you of something?' I asked.

'Yeah, well I must admit, it reminds me of the last party Pete had up here,' he replied. 'I think most of us were in a condition similar to the bees. Don't worry, Gwen, they will move off just before dawn. Any that are left will be harmless. And,' he smiled, 'tell Grandpa not to put that stuff outside!'

'That stuff' was bottled and sent home with the pickers. We made six hundred and fifty bottles of plum jam over the next three weeks. Pippin, the little farm stall on the Main Road, sold all of them over time and took orders for the next season. Everyone wanted more of it, because it wasn't too sweet.

The next season of jam-making on a commercial scale did not happen, because it didn't need to. I found another pack-shed, just opened and run by Richard. He paid within fifteen days instead of three months. He sold off the rejects to the traders for good prices and credited our account with the proceeds. I did make jam again, but only for the house and the staff, and as gifts.

13

Accident with the Tractor

It is Friday afternoon. Payday, 4 p.m. It is the fruit-picking season, and we are all tired. We stand outside the house in the yard. I give everyone their pay envelopes. They open their envelopes and repay me the week's borrowings, which we all know will be borrowed again by Tuesday.

They have worked very well this week. From 3 p.m. on Fridays is *skoonmaaktyd*. The lawn around the house is cut, paths are swept, gutters cleaned out, windows washed, the driveway gravel raked.

We move down to the *volkshuisies*, pick up all the rubbish dropped around the dustbins, and put it into the clearly marked rubbish drums, which are standing empty, then sweep all the verandas and paths. The children are out of school.

Parents use casual obscenities to their children as endearments, all delivered in screams or loud voices. I never get used to this, and query it.

'Nay, merrim, they are used to it, we are not cross with them.'

'Het jou Ma so gepraat, Dinie?' I ask.

'Of course, it's how we speak.'

The children push wheelbarrows, yell, fight, get in the way. They also have simple tasks to do, for which they get pocket money, then put away all the tools.

'I will see you on Monday morning,' says I hopefully.

'Ja, merrim, we will all be there,' they say together.

Saturday, 6 a.m. Very loud rapping on the window. 'Merrim, come quickly, there is an accident.' A woman's voice tells me this. I lie stupefied, swimming towards consciousness but wanting to think I am still asleep. The knocking goes on. 'Merrim, are you awake? You must come now!' It's Dinie, the housemaid.

I pull on the soiled clothes from the day before and go to find her. She is waiting at the kitchen door. 'It's the tractor, merrim. He is lying upside down, and there is somebody under.'

'Wie is onder die trekker, Dinie?' I ask as we walk down the vineyards.

'It's my neef, merrim,' she says, somewhat shamefaced. Her cousin does not work for me, and never has. I had put the tractor in the shed myself last evening after they had all left. I explain this to her very slowly.

She speaks quickly. 'Well, you see, merrim, he came to visit us late last night, and he was too drunk to walk to our house, so he saw the key in the ignition, and then he climbed on the tractor, en daar by ons huis hy het nie sy draai gekry en die trekker het oorgeval.' She sniffs a long drawn-out, wet sniff.

We get to the *volkshuisies* where a fair crowd has gathered, in spite of it being a Saturday and everyone not working. Entertainment is in short supply on the farms, at least the kind that is free, so the neighbouring staff had come to have a bit of fun.

I am seething with rage. Her cousin is a man of impenetrable stupidity, a drunken layabout I am going to strangle, or I must call the police to restrain me before I do. All kinds of hopelessly exaggerated deaths I could inflict on him run through my mind.

There is much laughter and camaraderie in the vineyard, and children are spinning the tractor wheels, which are up in the air. The tractor is balanced on both sides of an irrigation ditch, in which, sprawled on his back, is the cousin. He is incapable of getting up, he has wet his pants, and he is droolingly good-natured. He greets me effusively while supine in the ditch.

I have lots of language to draw on. My mother was descended from the Huguenot Pinards, now called Pienaars. They were sturdy peasants from Normandy. They turned up in Franschhoek in 1683. The family were all of farming stock for the first 160 years in South Africa. Three of my mother's sisters were married to farmers. We spoke and were educated in English, due to the deplorable fact of my mother's marriage to a foreigner whose family was from England. All the family gatherings, which took place virtually each weekend, were held in a jumble of English and Afrikaans, used in the vernacular, so by osmosis I had a muscular vocabulary of swearwords for emergencies. Something brought on by tiredness, aggravation and one stupidity too many surged through me. I exploded with rage.

I started with insults to the cousin's intelligence, or lack of it. I insulted his drinking habits, state of hygiene, manners, mental capacity and his appearance. The crowd stepped back a pace. I continued with his manhood, his morals, ethics, religion, support for the wrong rugby club, his skewed politics, and taste in refreshment. The crowd was now completely silent.

I took on his parentage and insulted every generation back to Jan van Riebeeck in Africa and the ones in Asia back to Genghis Khan. At this point I thought that I had said enough to intimidate everyone, and we could get on with a bit of damage control. I looked around.

Members of the public had made themselves comfortable on the ground. Half the Dendy-Young staff were there, egging me on. Children were hushed and still. They were all looking expectant. I heard some sibilant whispers, and realised that I was being assessed and getting marks for performance. According to the onlookers, I was just warming up.

To stop now would get me no credit at all. I thought about Shakespeare, with 'Bubble, bubble, toil and trouble', which didn't seem appropriate. A bit from *King John* might do, the Bastard at end of Act V Scene 3: 'Indeed your drums, being beaten, will cry out;/And so shall you, being beaten. Do but start/An echo with the clamour of thy drum.' No, I decided, that had the right idea, but was too brief to make the impression I wanted.

My Shakespeare had lapsed for a while, but ingrained daily readings of the Bible for the first twelve years of my life might provide something with which to entertain the audience. After all, the Bible contains many, many imprecations of the old-fashioned kind, the hell-and-damnation kind – not all this *si-kologee*, as my staff called it, that tells you everything is your mother's fault. These laws, these commandments, were strong enough down history to put millennia of sinners off Alcohol, Thieving, Murder, Idleness, Cheating, Lies, Gluttony and Adultery. Not all of them, but some of them.

I stop my speculations at that moment, because out of the trees around the dam two girls come into sight, riding horses in the translucent morning light. The horse in the front is a light grey, with a beautiful head. He is just the inspiration I need. Thank you, Angels, that will do nicely: Revelation 6: 8. 'And I looked, and behold a pale horse: and his name that sat on him was Death, and Hell followed with him. And power was given unto them over the fourth part of the earth, to kill with sword, and with hunger, and with death, and with the beasts of the earth.'

That is the perfect opening to a recitation of earthquakes; the sun going black; the moon, should I ask it, turning to blood. The sinner who took my tractor will have to hide in caves from my vengeance, and his children will not call him father. His wives and concubines will mock him and all be unfaithful to him. Rocks will be raining down on him from the heavens. I describe in detail the horrors when he goes to hell, and a thousand years thereafter. Oh, the punishments, the thirst, the starvations, the flayings. No priest could have shown more graphically to him the error of his ways. I am giving a performance which would have been a credit to Sarah Bernhardt.

Most of the audience is enthralled. Some of the more bleary-eyed men are looking uncomfortable. It is Saturday morning, the morning after the night before, and Friday nights are party nights. There is the evidence of this lying in the ditch, from whence, in that moment's silence, there is a sound of a wheezing, rattling breath. The son of all jackals is crying noisily.

The bastard, he is crying, I think. I should be crying. What if the tractor was damaged and we could not get it going? How were we to get the fruit down to the pack-shed?

A loud wail issues from the ditch. 'Ag, ek is jammer, merrim, o merrim, sorry, I am so sorry.' I don't acknowledge him.

'Jinne, Miz Gwen, waar het jy daaie verskriklike woorde geleer?' the maid asks, pop-eyed.

'From the time I got to this bloody farm,' I reply furiously.

'Ag asseblief, little merrim, don't disturb yourself,' several people say at once. 'We will get the tractor back on his wheels.' And with that, the more sturdy of the spectators start to rock the tractor.

The cousin crawls out of the ditch, wiping vomit and snot down his trouser leg. Once upright, the trekker still treks. But we have to replace thirteen vines, eight poles and fifty metres of wire.

85

Four women, with some children, accompany Dinie and me up to the kitchen to have breakfast and make some decent coffee. They ask me sheepishly if I might come and give a 'talk' like that to their husbands once in a while when discipline breaks down over the weekend. I decline. Some things you just can't encore.

14

Dinie's Baby

It was 31 December. The blinding heat of the day was cooling slightly. The pack-shed had closed at 2 p.m. The staff had been paid, and a weekend lay ahead.

We had been picking fruit for six weeks and were all exhausted. I made my usual self-defence speech to the assembly, about thirty strong. 'Now look, you have got your money and your medicine, and I don't want to see anyone here before Tuesday, do you understand me?'

It was a rhetorical question. 'Ja natuurlik, merrim,' they agreed in unison, knowing the delusion we were all practising.

I walked up to the house and into the bathroom, pulling off the sticky dusty clothing as I went. The bathroom tiles felt cool under my tired feet. Later I lay in the bath for a long time, contemplating the joy of peace and quiet and a pleasant evening …

The television had announced that at 6 p.m. one could join Kirk Douglas, who was the guide at the Jeu de Paume in Paris, for a personal tour of the Impressionists. I had read somewhere that he himself had a magnificent art collection including a large number of these artists. Who better, then, to be a guide? The prospect of this glimpse into a more refined world, and then supper and champagne on the terrace, filled me with pleasure. Life could be worse. Very shortly it was.

I had washed my hair, tidied myself up and put on a thin cotton kaftan, switched on the telly and made myself comfortable on the bed. Kirk Douglas and I were gazing at 'The Waterlilies'. Sublime, they were. Some of the colours reminded me of the mountains down the Valley in the dawn light.

Bill, who was in the kitchen, comes into the bedroom. 'There is someone at the back door for you,' he says.

'How come it is never for you?' I ask through my teeth. He has not spent the day in the heat. His sole self-proclaimed duty is to drive the fully loaded tractor down to the pack-shed, and drive it back.

'Oh Gwen, you know I don't speak the language. Besides it's a child.'

'Well, tell them I'm not here. I'm in Paris with a handsome man, and I am not coming back ever.'

He looks at me. You know that expressionless stare that people exchange when they can't be bothered to start a fight. It's no good asking why 35 years' residence in South Africa has not equipped him with a basic level of the official languages. I go to the back door.

It is the maid's eleven-year-old daughter. 'Merrim,' she says, 'my Ma sê jy moet kom!'

'Why, for what reason?' says I.

'Nay, merrim, weet nie.' She looks at her toes making patterns in the sand, and waits, head hanging.

88

'Gaan uitvind! I am not going to walk all that way without knowing why I must come.'

'Ja, merrim, ek sal haar so sê.' She skips out of sight.

Kirk Douglas has not waited for me. He is standing in front of a Degas. We marvel together at that gossamer pink of the girls' tutus, the slanting light of Paris coming into the dancers' studio, the luminescence of a young girl's uplifted arms. I am engrossed in the painter's technique in putting emotions of ambition, poise and disappointment, exhaustion and loneliness, on the canvas.

Bill appears at the door. 'Uh, Gwen, the child is back,' he says, and walks away.

I go to the kitchen. The child, face anxious, says, 'My Ma sê sy dink die baba kom.'

Oh, hell and damnation, of all things! The baby is not expected for another three weeks.

'Has your father called the ambulance?' I ask

'Weet nie, merrim,' she says, while looking at me with perplexity on her narrow child's face.

'Nou kyk, daar is 'n klomp vroue met jou Ma. Jou Ouma is daar, your two Aunties, two neighbours, and your father. They have a telephone, and they can phone the ambulance, and so will I. They must just wait a little bit longer.'

'Ja, merrim,' she says, and goes off. I phone Paarl Emergency. They will be here in half an hour. I go back to Kirk Douglas, with whom I am now seriously in love. He is threading his way down to Van Gogh.

I think I know why Kirk does this to me. Once the picking starts in Franschhoek, a curious aberration overtakes all the inhabitants. Style goes out of the window. Hair does not get trimmed, not everyone remembers to shave in the morning, for days at a time. Fingernails are broken, socks sag, pants don't stay up. Buttons pop off and are not replaced. Overalls do not get washed, shoes are not polished, language takes a turn for the worse. It is all blamed on the fruit season.

It is rumoured that once the men are out of the house, wives leap into any vehicles available to see divorce lawyers in Stellenbosch, Paarl and even Cape Town. One wife was so desperate, she took the farm tractor, but having never driven one before, she didn't get further than the railway crossing and was found by an extremely irate husband, lying unharmed in a ditch, with no ambition to get up or go home. When he asked what the hell she was doing, she told him she was lying in the ditch because it was more peaceful than home, and so far no one had shouted at her. I might be the only person who believed this story. Any place, during the fruit season, was more peaceful than home.

In this environment, a truly well-dressed and groomed man looks, well, tasty. Kirk Douglas was not just well dressed: Savile Row would have wept with joy. Oh, the cloth of his suit, the way it fitted into his waist, the spotless Italian shirt and silk tie, his haircut, the gleaming shoes. His underwear, I knew, would be of the best – silky things that slithered off. I was just speculating on how he might, uhm, look without all his clothing, when Bill appears once more.

'The child is back again,' says he.

I try to explain to Kirk, These things happen, just wait for me – but he doesn't listen and is away down the corridor to Gauguin. Giving in to inevitability, off goes the kaftan, on go the dirty jeans, T-shirt, farm shoes.

I follow the child down to the house, which I notice is very quiet. Dinie opens the door for me, munching a piece of toast. 'Where is everyone, Dinie?' I ask.

'O, Miz Gwen, dis goed om jou te sien. I sent the Oumas away with the children to the dam to go and play. Andries, my husband, is standing at the top of the farm by the other dam to wave to the ambulance when they come.'

She makes me a cup of tea. We talked of the peach prices, the new Dominee at the church, her mother's arthritis, the children's school reports, the latest episode of *Dallas*, the price of school socks at the local haberdasher: everything except the reason for my presence.

Suddenly she puts her teacup down. 'Miz Gwen, ek gaan stoot.' She is looking into my eyes with an occupied expression.

'No, for God's sake, Dinie, do not push,' I say desperately. 'They are on their way, Dinie, the ambulance people, just hang on for five minutes.'

The next moment, she flings her arms about me, squeezing me for grim death and panting into my ear. It is like the embrace of a pregnant python. I think I hear one of my ribs crack. This is a lady who can pick up two crates fully packed with fruit and casually throw them onto the tractor. Together they weigh sixty pounds.

'Is die pyn, merrim, is die pyn!' she whimpers, tightening her grip.

'Dinie, let me go, I can't help you like this.' I prise her hands loose.

'I feel like going to the toilet,' she says.

'No, no.' I am yelling. 'Don't go in there, the baby will drown,' I say, leaping in front of her and locking the door. I put the key in my pocket and turn to where she is standing.

Long ago I had been called out by my mother on a dark frosty morning in Johannesburg to deliver a child of my own housemaid, who was staying in one of our unused farm buildings until her confinement. She had, inexplicably and silently, been impregnated by the butcher's delivery man walking into the kitchen and out again. It wasn't even a large order and I was in the next room at the time. I also had some small store of knowledge of this birth process, having given birth to three sons.

I look at Dinie closely. Oh hell. Oh hell!!!! 'Kneel on the floor and push, Dinie.' Under her, I bundle a few dishcloths that I have grabbed off the sink. I sit on the floor in front of her, holding onto her body to steady her through the force of her contractions.

She screams once, a low primordial howl from the back of the throat. The tendons in her neck stand out like ropes. She is going to have this baby right now, and nothing is going to stop her. A convulsion of pain and muscular contraction rolls down her body, then water, blood, membranes and baby all arrive together.

She lies down on the floor gasping. I feel like joining her, but I pick up the baby and lay him in her arms. He is perfectly made. I look at the scrunched little face to make sure all is well, and there are the two ears, two eyes, a button nose, and a wide mouth just opening to give his first shout of life. The umbilical cord is still pulsing, and below it I see he has the necessary equipment to re-create himself one day.

At that moment, two scrubbed and very businesslike chaps came through the door. They waved me out of the way and took over. I was pleased about that. I walked out of the room and sat on an overturned dustbin because I couldn't walk any further, my legs were shaking so much. The evening star was shining directly over-head. I know why I started to cry. I am not unsusceptible to miracles.

Later, Dinie was carried out on a stretcher, smiling and smiling. The baby, fists clenched, was in a tiny carry-cot. His name was Thomas, called after Dinie's father.

I walked slowly back to the house through the rich purple twi-light. The strains of 'Joy to the World' greeted me when I climbed up the veranda steps. The night air felt soft and the sky looked in-finite. Every star there ever was, was shining brightly. To hell with Paris, it was wonderful right here.

15

Paulina's Story

I was born in 1942 on La Bri farm. My parents were Willem and Hannie Daniels. The owners of the farm were Phillip and Bettie Hugo. Pa Hugo was the *jongman*. His father was still farming.

I was the sixth child of fourteen children. We had a house of four rooms, boys in one room, girls in the other, and Ma and Pa in another with the smallest children. I was one of those who slept in the room, for my first years, with my parents. The other big room was kitchen, dining-room and living-room.

The house had a *mis* floor of dung. Every Friday morning we children went out to collect the dry pats of *mis* into buckets. We also went to the river, to collect clay. There was a clay border or rim around the rooms. If it was broken anywhere, we had to fix it.

I think a lot of boys became plasterers because of the skills they got from fixing their mothers' floors. The *mis* was soaked in water and mixed with a bit of paraffin. It was smoothed over the floor everywhere, up to the clay edging, and left to dry. Then when it was dry we took floor polish and made it shine. It had a smell of herbs and fresh grass. I liked it very much. It had a soft shine in the sun, and was quite hard-wearing.

Saturday afternoon was for baking bread. My big brother was the one who baked it, in the oven outside. He had to get the fire just right. He chose all different woods from around the farm and along the river. He said that different woods made the bread taste different. My mother was busy in the kitchen, kneading all the dough in one great mound. She had very strong arms from the years of doing this. Then, when all the pans were standing full of the dough for the bread to rise again, we had to be very careful not to open a door in case the bread got cold and fell down. It was my big brother's right to have the first slice off one of the loaves, and he would sit in the kitchen eating the bread and drinking coffee with my mother while the little ones slept. If that was happening in the kitchen, then I knew my world was perfectly safe.

Oh, the smell of that bread out of the coal oven, and the wonderful wheat, freshly ground, tasting of the sun, makes my mouth water. The fresh cold butter that I had churned, that smelled a bit sour from the buttermilk, melted into it. That was such good food, it is enough to make you cry. But also you see, Miz Gwen, it is not just the bread, but with it all the things I remember, and the family I loved, gathered around the table, and so many of them are gone now.

All the children went to the Weseind school that went up to Standard 6. At thirteen I left school to stay and help my mother with the smaller children. I did that until I was fourteen, and then got a job with some brown people. I was doing all the washing and looking after children. I was still living at home. Then I got work in the vineyards on La Bri, *stokkies optel* and other farm jobs like packing boxes of fruit for export. It was four months of very hard work in the year.

My mother's much younger sister also worked on La Bri. She did all the thinning of the peaches. She had long hands and thin fingers. Her fingers used to fly up the branches, and the little peaches would be dropping on the ground. She always left just the right number on the trees, and they were the very best peaches. She was a magic woman at this job. She never looked at what she was doing, her hands had their own knowledge of what to take off, and she used to walk along the rows, talking and laughing, and everything was always perfectly done. The farmers used to take her to the farms all over the Valley to show the other staff how to do this.

She said she had got a boyfriend, but we never saw him. Then she was pregnant. The baby was a girl child, born early in the evening and very light-coloured. The next morning my Oupa, who had just got out of jail the night before, was very, very angry. He told the family that before he came back from work, the baby must be thrown into the pigs' stalls to be eaten by them.

Women are givers of life, and we could not obey him. We were much frightened, but we made a plan and did it straightaway. We asked this baby to be still, very still. Then right under Oupa's nose, like the baby Moses in the bulrushes, the baby was carried out of the house in a basket. A few nappies were covering the baby, an empty tea packet and a half-finished packet of biscuits were also in the basket as a camouflage.

'Ag, Oupa, we are just going to have tea next door,' we sisters said. We ran to take the last bakkie going from the village to Paarl. We got off at the corner of the Helshoogte Pass road near Boschendal and walked to our Auntie's cottage. Auntie lived in Languedoc. She was a woman with wide arms and a large heart. She brought up the baby like her own daughter, and the mother was not allowed to see her at all. Only after Auntie died, the mother could only see her child as another Auntie and she was not allowed to say, This is my child. The baby girl is married now. She is beautiful. She has three sons, but she is quiet with you, you can't stop her quiet even by laughing.

La Bri also had sheep and horses and cows. They used to graze all over the town and out on the hills. For the winter grazing, all the sheep and cows went with the other grazing animals to Oudebosch near Langebaan. They left in April, after Easter. The walk took five days. The farmers from Franschhoek had bought lots of old farms there, and made big grazing lands. My father, Willem, would collect all the cattle from La Bri and he would walk in front of all of the farmers' cattle, or he would ride a lovely white horse called Blue.

He told us all a story about having to go up the mountain to gather the cows together. They took their time, but later they were all ready to go except one. She was standing a little way away, behind a rock. My father called and called, but she didn't move. My father went right up to the cow, and he saw something he had never seen before. A young farmer was lying on the ground, sucking the cow's teat, and masturbating at the same time. My Pa was kind to him and let him finish, because everyone in the Valley knew that his mother had died birthing him, and if he took his comfort from a cow, what was there to say?

One day when the men did not come back for lunch, my father asked me to lead the white horse, Blue, while he was ploughing. I loved that horse, he was beautiful and held his head so proudly. I was very gentle with him, and my father was so pleased with me that I worked with him for the rest of the ploughing season.

The ploughing started after good rains, and you know, Miz Gwen, it used to rain for fourteen days without stopping. It doesn't happen like that any more. Also every winter, the snow lay thick on the mountains, and many years the snow was right along the main road. We thought that was wonderful. We would wrap cloth around our hands and throw snowballs, and if there was a little hill we could slide on a piece of flat wood and have such fun.

I also remember after the Big War, there was an Italian prisoner of war called Sabatoni who came in 1943. He was the foreman for Koos Hugo at La Bri. We all used to steal grapes to eat. He got a pellet gun and filled it with coarse salt, and shot at us. *Jislaaik*, it used to sting, and he would shout at us, 'Scram!' I don't know where he learned that word. He liked the coloured girls very much. He called them *amore* and they asked him why he used the same name for every girl. He was always trying to 'love' them.

In 1947 the King and Queen came to visit. She was on all the money, the pounds, and five pounds, and ten pounds. We listened to the King speaking on the radio. Do you know a radio licence was three shillings for the year?

One day when I was fourteen years old, I started to bleed between my legs, and I asked a friend to help me. I was afraid to tell my mother – she shouted a lot. She had never told me anything about this. My friend told me how to put a white cloth between my legs, and to change the cloths. Also, that when the bleeding stopped, to put the cloths in Jik, and then they would be ready for the next time I bled when it was full moon. She said that, just like the moon getting full, my body would get full, and then it had to empty itself, so the blood would come out again. This happened to all girls at my age, and from this time on I must not let a boy touch me, otherwise I would have a baby.

That night, before I went into the house, I stood outside and looked up at the moon. It was full moon, and so the next month I watched the moon, and when it was full I started to bleed again.

My parents didn't want any of us girls to have a boyfriend, so the boys didn't come to the front door. They tapped on the back window, and sometimes we climbed out there, and we went and *vryed* in the bush. It was just kissing and feeling.

My Auntie was very funny. She took an old pillow, and she cut and stitched it into the shape of a head and shoulders. She painted on a face, and sewed on black wool to look like hair. When you got out of bed you put this pillow into your bed, and if your Pa came to look with the candle he thought it was you sleeping there.

I had a boyfriend. After I got my periods I told him we couldn't hold hands because I would have a baby. He said, 'Oh God, so now I can't touch you, because you have been bleeding. You are not a little girl any more, but a woman.' He was very romantic, he used to write me notes every day and leave them at the gate under a *bossie*. He brought me flowers on Fridays. Then he kissed me. It felt like the time I put my finger in the light socket.

My mother said that kissing gave you babies. When my boyfriend was sixteen he got a job with a fishmonger. They used to deliver fish to the farms, and he used to throw me a fish off the back of the lorry. He lost his job because the fisherman said he was stealing fish.

I was nineteen, nearly twenty, when I first had sex. I liked the boy very much, and I was curious about sex. He said that he loved me. He told me that all girls had to be 'broken' for the first time and it would hurt me, but that he would try to be gentle. I asked him what we had to do. It was a very hot afternoon, by the river, and I remember the sun shining onto the water, and the trembling that was in my body. I remember, too, he reached out his hand very slowly and softly, and took off my earrings; then with the same slow softness, he unbuttoned my blouse, and touched my breasts. It was very sore, that thing he did the first time, but after that for me sex was wonderful. I stayed with the first boyfriend, but then I found out he was also loving another girl, so I didn't want him any more. A week later, another boy that I knew from the Christmas choir asked me if he could be my boyfriend. I had known him for a long time, and I said, Yes, why not?

What was very nice was when we told ghost stories. We would sit close together, and when we got frightened we could hold onto the one next to us. There were a lot of stories on the radio, and then Ouma would also tell us stories she had heard when she was a child.

There was a man called Jakob in the Valley, and he was a bad man. Because we didn't have electricity or tap water, the girls had to go and fetch it from the dam or the rivers, and sometimes it was in the dark. On this evening a little girl fetched water, and when she got home there was a frog in the bucket, and her mother threw it away. So she went a second time, and when she got into the kitchen she saw there was a snake in it. So she had to go again, and while she was there, Jakob and another man killed this girl.

Quite soon after that, when we went to get water she would walk past, dressed like a bride. At first we were scared, but afterwards we said her name and told her about her family. She only once looked around, and smiled, and then we did not see her again.

Sometimes, Miz Gwen, when you walk down the road past Champagne to go to the bridge, you will see leaves blowing behind you, and then they follow you across the bridge, and it is funny because there is no wind at all. Some people have been followed all the way to the village. I think that ghost must be a man, because he only likes to follow the women.

The Christmas choir was organised by Giepie and Miz Sarie le Roux. We practised for months, and then on Christmas Eve we used to sing all over Franschhoek. We sang first at La Bri, which had been called Keervlei – the farmer was Abraham Das. Then at La Dauphine for Seppie Malherbe, then La Colline, then we went to Little Champagne, and then to Excelsior. Oupa Maskie and his wife were the most loving and kind people, and always so generous to us. Then we went all the way round by Robertsvlei.

We were thirty people in the choir and we sang all night. We walked from farm to farm, and it was early in the morning of Christmas Day when we got home. All the people left us sweets, cake and cool drinks. Sometimes we would get a little money. Some of the farmers opened the cellars for us and we had a *doppie*, but then at one farm half the choir didn't come out of the cellar at all until the next morning. It was the boys and the men, of course.

When I was with the boy from the choir, he sang to me. The songs he sang were so wonderful and full of love, I got pregnant. I was 21 years old. But at four months, I miscarried. It was a little girl. She was so small I tried to hold her hand, and for a moment she closed her tiny hand around my little finger, then she was gone. I cried for a long time. The boyfriend left me after that – I didn't see him again.

When I was 26 I met another man who was only known by his initials, EAJ Williams. We got married. He worked, and I stayed at home. He was nice to me in the beginning, but he was a real *joller*. I was pregnant again, but miscarried at five months. The doctor said it was a fallopian pregnancy. The baby was a son. I thought maybe he would be there when I was old, but he also gave one tiny puff of breath, and he was gone. I got divorced and sterilised, and went back to Franschhoek. For a long time after that, I felt I was not a woman, and was lonely and alone.

Franschhoek was a dirty town then. The main road was tarred but none of the other roads; they were just sand or mud in the winter. There was no rubbish collection. All the packets and papers that people threw down at the shops blew all over the *dorp* when the winds came, and the shops were dirty. Also, in the main road nobody painted the shops, and the dust and heat and flies in the summer were terrible. There were no visitors and everyone went to Paarl for the big shopping. It was a poor *dorpie*, lonely and far from everything.

I got a job with Mrs Rykie Michelson. She was a lovely lady. Mrs Michelson, Jan Roux, Koos Hugo and Pieter Haumann were all town councillors. Jan Roux used to visit Mrs Michelson to talk about plans for Franschhoek. That's when I used to listen to them. He said he wanted to be a building contractor. Then he would build some nice buildings in Franschhoek. He wanted a memorial for the Huguenots, and a museum, and also a building for the winery. They chose the land carefully and made plans. So that is what he did, he was very determined that the Huguenots will not be forgotten. They were his ancestors. It took a long time, but he was very careful to do it all right. He studied a lot of plans and thought how the place should look when people came from far away to see it.

When the earthquake came in 1969, it broke dam walls, which washed away some vineyards, and it broke the walls of the church. Mr Jan was there and he fixed it all up, and the church was beautiful again. Then more people went back to church, and it was used for concerts and also music recitals. Then he was asked to go and fix all the old houses in the Boland, and people were very happy. He taught a lot of coloured men to do really good work, so that they could also start their own businesses.

Did you know, Miz Gwen, that the farmers used to give each other funny names, because in some of the very big old Huguenot families there would be two or three generations with the same traditional names, and if you talked about them no one would know which one it was? There were many of the Hugos and the men were nicknamed Koos. There was Klomp Koos, and Robertsvlei Koos, and Koos La Colline, and Koos Winkel, and Koos Kop. Then many of the Le Rouxs were called Ganse. These were the Le Rouxs who came from Blois in France, so they were called Blois Ganse; another Môreson Ganse – the attached name would be their farm names and then everyone knew who they were. Other family names were just funny names, like Willie Meerkat, Trap-in-die-Gaatjie, Lang Jan, Wit Jan, Jan Pypies, Klein Jan.

There was a man called Koue Kookwater. He always used to say, 'O, nou kook ek, I am boiling,' but he never boiled in his life – he was timid and quiet, that is how he got his name. There were many generations of Patat, like Jan Patat, who was Jan Roux, the builder. And all the Goedehoop Rouxs. One of the school teachers was called Snow White because she had lovely fair hair and very pale skin, and Mary was Little Red Riding Hood because she loved wearing red. One of the Du Toits up on your farm, Patrysfontein, was called Vol Baklei because that was how he was, he was never in a good mood. Other families were called Die Meerkatte, or Skilpad, or Ostriches, or Murgbeen if they were long and thin like a string-bean, and when you looked at them, Miz Gwen, you knew why they had those names.

Dr Isaac lived on the Pass Road. He was a huge man, like some giant, six feet eight inches. *Jirre*, he was tall, and he took size twelve shoes. He was the only doctor who visited everyone, whatever their colour. Brown and white, he got angry if you were in need and you didn't call him to see a sick person. If you couldn't pay, then he didn't even ask. He delivered a lot of babies, and in those days children's eyes did not open for the first ten days. You had to lie in bed with the baby for that time. The Dokter came each day and treated the mother with antiseptic between her legs, to heal properly. Then it was a special time on the tenth day when you got out of bed and put on a dress, and that day the baby would open its eyes for the first time.

Ballroom dancing was one of the ways we had fun. There were people who used to come up every Saturday night from District Six, where the coloureds and Muslims lived in Cape Town, and bring their wives and their musical instruments. They played the guitar, saxophone, clarinet, accordion, flute, viola, bass, penny whistle, concertina and mouth organs.

After the dance, they would go to different farms to spend the night, and right there in the moonlight behind the houses one player would play with all his heart, sometimes until it got light. Those men who played, I could see they were *opgelig* in the music and could have floated up into the sky on their own notes.

I loved the saxophone: it seemed to speak to me in a special voice. I could see the long drawn-out notes of it going up through the trees in spirals of silver. There were many of those nights we sat under the great trees and listened to the musicians until dawn. Oh, Miz Gwen, it was like magic. To see the shadowed mountain, the stars and the moonlight, you felt protected, as if nothing bad could ever happen.

We were the best dancers, my sisters and me, because our father, Willem, was the dancing instructor. The Kamrick Hall was used on

Saturday nights for the dancing, and during the week my father gave lessons there on Wednesday nights. He was allowed to have the key. Oh, how I loved it. I could dance for four hours without sitting down at all.

I was very thin, and had a few lovely dresses which my mother made for all of us. Nearly the best was when we went to the shops to buy the fabric. I loved taffeta, the way it shone and crackled. My dresses had little straps over the shoulders, tight bodices, and a full-circle skirt. We wore a petticoat underneath the dress that was stiffly starched. The petticoats were made of cotton with lace around the hem, and when they were starched they could stand up by themselves in the corner of the room.

I was the one who opened the dancing with my father, so the other people could see how to waltz or foxtrot or quickstep, and then we would also close the dancing with the last dance. I felt very proud of myself, and sometimes then I also felt that I was beautiful.

One of our traditions was that, before the last dance, four boys would reach out their hands to each other and hold hands, two together. The four of them with arms outstretched would ask a girl to lie across their arms, and they would throw her up into the air and catch her. This was great fun, and they never dropped one of us. On one evening, a girl who had not come dancing before was asked, and she lay down across their arms. She was very thin and so she flew up into the air and so did all her skirts, and *merrim, daar was haar poephol, kaal en nakend,* she had forgotten to put on her *broeks.*

Later I got a job at Champagne, and I packed wood-wool into the boxes for the export peaches. I packed it very carefully so that on their journey all across the sea the peaches would not get hurt. When my father was working late in the fruit season, he would come home with boxes of *uitval* and he would say, 'Those who are not asleep can come and eat some fruit,' and we would all come running out to eat the wonderful fruit.

I am much older now, but I remember those days and the family. I remember how it was simple, and we had little, but every day God gave us was a day to live and enjoy, and help and be together. Now sometimes I wish it could be like that again, because something more than just those days has disappeared from our lives.

16

Snakes and Other Dangerous Beasts

I had been in and out of the house most of the day. It was one of those warm spring days, with the promise of resurrection in the air after a long and cold winter. It was vibrating with life, growth and all kinds of enticements. A group of women were working in the top vineyard close to the house. Suddenly there was yelling and screaming, high-pitched clustered noises. Running towards them, I asked what the matter was.

''n Slang, 'n slang, daar's hy, merrim,' they said in unison. Weeds and dry grasses from the previous season were parted and there, folded in on himself, lay a tiny snake with bright eyes. The darker outline of his mouth seemed to be pulled up into a smile. He was all of fifteen centimetres long and not much thicker than a pencil.

'Ag, julle is so pieperig! Just get him out of the way,' I said. From the noise they made I was expecting something much bigger.

'Miz Gwen, jy is mal. Hy sal ons doodbyt, ons vat nie aan sulke dinge nie.' I had heard them say the same things about chameleons, crickets, dung beetles and a great variety of insects. Spiders were the most hated.

I took a fork and touched the snake with one of the tines. He moved away slowly and I grabbed him firmly behind the neck and held him up. He looked like a fat strand of macaroni, mottled with olives. I carried him over to the bushes near the fence between the Dendy-Youngs' and our farm, and put him down to do whatever it is that baby snakes do. Work was resumed, with much talk of *slang* stories.

Towards the late afternoon I went out to assess progress and paint a new wall, which enclosed a section of the garden recently terraced and planted. I set to work, chattering to the women at the same time. I heard the tractor coming from the bottom of the farm, and I needed to give the driver instructions for the following day. I was standing on the dirt road barefoot, waiting for the driver, Kobus, to come closer to me so that we could speak.

The steering wheel of the tractor was turned towards me. He was staring fixedly at something in the road and seemed oblivious of the fact that if he continued he would flatten both me and the new wall. I started jumping up and down and waving my arms at him to stop, but he didn't notice. 'Pas op, merrim!' the women were yelling. Bugger that, I thought, how do I stop this cretin from bashing my new wall and me to smithereens? At the very last minute he turned the wheel and stopped the tractor twenty centimetres from me.

'Jirre tog, wat maak jy, Kobus? Is jy blind?' I shouted at him. He leaned forward slowly and put his elbows on the steering wheel. 'Merrim, het jy jou Bybel gelees?' he asked me with the withering disapproval of a puritanical missionary.

'Read my Bible, Kobus?' I was bewildered.

'Kyk na jou voete,' he said. I looked down. There, between my bare feet, lay the brother of the little snake, or if it was Little Snake himself, he had Olympic potential for covering long distances. Besides the Serpent in the Garden of Eden and his enticements to Eve, I couldn't quite see his point.

Kobus took a deep breath and continued. 'Slange was die begin van al die probleme in die wêreld, merrim. God het ons gesê dat ons hulle almal moet doodmaak, anders sal hy jou in jou haksteen byt, merrim' – here he raised his eyebrows, then continued – 'en dan,' he paused, 'is jy onder die grond in.' He paused again, for dramatic effect. 'Unnerground, in jou kis, merrim!' He articulated each word slowly and most precisely, and his hooded eyes invited me to look at my death. He sat back in the tractor seat, arms now folded across his chest, full of righteousness.

What do we have here, I wondered, scrutinising him. His face was curiously blank, the expression in his eyes not unlike the fanatical gleam of religious extremists. In detail, I looked at his hands. The short stumpy fingers with broad spatulate nails were like primitive tools. Those hands would be eager to take things from others that were not on offer. They would claw unripe fruit off the trees, they would twist the necks of birds not yet grown.

Suddenly the tension which I had been keenly aware of between father and daughter was clearer than ever. These emotionally impotent men who deprive their own daughters of the hope of a secure childhood by their sexual attacks on them within a home have to be the lowest form of life on the planet. I knew about him, in that moment, with absolute clarity, and what went on in the family cottage at night. Maria had made oblique references to 'trouble' but would never say what it was. Righteousness was not an ethic in which he could take refuge.

I looked down at my feet. The brother of Little Snake had, during this oration, taken the opportunity to hide in a large clump of violets close by, and I could see a tiny tail just visible under the leaves. I took a very deep breath, and my fury, which had long been simmering inside me at what I knew of his behaviour, erupted. I didn't pause to think.

'Laat my jou iets sê, Kobus,' I said slowly, confident that the grammatical shortcomings of the Afrikaans in which I generally communicated with the staff were the least of my worries. 'Al die probleme in die wêreld is nie gemaak deur slange of ander diere, maar deur manne soos jy, who violate every decency of human behaviour. You are a drunk and a violent one! Jy slaan die vroumense in jou eie familie. Jy kan nie eers die slang in jou eie broek keer! As ek hoor dat jy jou vuil hande op jou dogter of jou niggie ooit weer gesit het, jy is onder die grond in, in jou kis, with the lid screwed down, and you will never get to see the light of day, ever again.'

'Jirre, Miz Gwen, versigtig nou, Miz Gwen, moenie so sê nie!' the women chorused from the field six metres away. They were clustered together in shock, hands covering their mouths in nervousness. They held the garden tools in front of their bodies as if to defend themselves. The habit of female conspiracy to keep silence was still deeply entrenched in our country.

It was not to be expected that cordial relations could be maintained between us after that incident, but we did not speak of it, avoided each other most of the time, and life carried on without further incident. The farm was later sold, and the staff stayed on with the new owner. A year later, we moved into our newly built house which adjoined the old farm, and Maria, the long-suffering wife, came to see me.

'Do you know what happened to Kobus?' she asked.

'No, how would I know? Tell me,' I said.

She looked at me for a long time, enjoying her secret before it would be shared. A wide satisfied smile spread across her face. She looked different, better, more feminine. Her smile was not the smile of a victim, but of someone who had won a battle.

'I nearly killed him,' she said softly, 'and now he is gone from us. I haven't seen him for more than a year. You know we have been to the hospital many times when he hit all of us, and the Dokter he said, just like merrim, "Make sure you hit him harder than he can hit you."' It was just what I had told her, after another weekend of violence from which there had been no protection.

The story went on. He had cornered her in the kitchen armed with a sturdy length of iron piping. He had been drinking most of the day, as he had done every weekend when in my employ. 'Vandag maak ek julle almal dood,' he said calmly. Certainly there was sufficient reason to believe him.

He had backed her into a corner by the stove, and against her leg she felt the chopper handle. She had put it there after chopping wood to light the stove. She picked it up and got in the first blow to his head, almost splitting his skull. The second blow cut through the bone of his left arm. She was a very strong woman, and in desperate circumstances.

He was still alive but had seemingly lost all further desire for spilling other blood, since his own was gushing copiously onto the kitchen floor.

He was rushed to Paarl Casualty, and the doctor had not wasted much sympathy on the biter being bitten. 'Why didn't you finish the bastard off while you were at it?' he asked Maria.

'Merrim, we are so happy now, the children are doing well at skool, and the teachers, they tell me it's much better with them. Also my daughter and the other one, they are not afraid any more. It's like some bad thing has gone from our lives.'

Rough but necessary justice had been done through a woman defending herself and her children. I, for one, could find nothing to judge in her actions, only query why it took so long.

17

The Constant Gardeners

While we lived on the top farm, a thin melancholy man came to ask for work. He had a long face, light-brown skin and those heavy-lidded, oval eyes that Giotto painted in the fourteenth century. It gave him a look of continual piety. He had beautiful hands, with very slender wrists. The fingers were long and tapered – the knuckles hardly interrupted the shape of them. They were the hands of a musician or an artist.

He wore a large woolly cap pulled over clearly visible dreadlocks. He sniffed, and appeared to be asthmatic. Fumes of marijuana scented the air around him. His name was Martin, and he was a Rastafarian. He lived with his sister Linkie and her husband, Ben, at the bottom of the farm road, past Uncle John Lotter's dam. I suggested that he might work for two days a week in the garden. It was agreed.

He arrived on the appointed day, punctual to the minute. He was diligent, silent and very professional. He knew what he was doing and he did it. At breakfast time I asked him if he was married. 'Nay, merrim, women causes men a lot of trouble. I go to my church, and I like to watch rugby.' Well, thinks I, he sounds nice and clean cut. Within the allotted time he had done more than most, and very well too.

Martin became a fixture in my life. The sad face could break into huge grins and laughter. He loved the dogs with a passion. Marijuana was therapeutic, he said, and necessary for a man's health. He despaired of the younger generation. He was an old man of 22. He loved his father Japie, and Japie's best friend, Peetie. He adored his mom, Maria, and she adored him. Linkie, his sister, was his best friend in the world.

We sold the farm three years later and rented the manor house on Chamonix – a large farm of mixed fruit and vines – for eight months, while we set about building operations. When it was possible to live in, we moved into the half-built house. This property was on an old title deed; probably the land had been rented for a nominal sum to some farmer for grazing his cows, and over time it became his and then ours. It was adjoining, but below, the previous farm. Martin stayed the course. Wherever we were, he was with us. He was, as John le Carré would say, a constant gardener.

He had become a great pal of my son Peter, who worked at the winery. They were the same age, 25 going on 40. Peter and Martin were rugby fanatics. It was 'Province or nothing'. Martin played for a Paarl rugby club, and one imagines the effect on the opposition as this tall thin man, with dreadlocks like the tail of a comet, rushed down the wing. If there was any match with Province at Newlands, Pete would get tickets, load up Martin and his friends in the bakkie, and off they would go. If Province actually won, then it was Mike's Kitchen, a steak house in Claremont for celebrations, and quite a lot of beer. If Province did not win, the conversation would take a turn for the worse. 'Who are these Aunties who are playing, en wie het hulle gisteraand genaai? See, they can't even run today.'

I had decided to get the new garden going soon after the house foundations were in. We started planting trees near the perimeter. We had lorryloads of pig and cow manure, collectable from Rhodes Dairy Farms at ten rands for a large load piled high. We needed more help. 'I will bring my father and Peetie on Saturday morning, merrim,' said Martin.

Since the two men were semi-retired I wasn't too hopeful. I went out to inspect the labour force the next morning. Three smiling faces greeted me. They introduced themselves. Japie was a shorter, older version of Martin, without the dreadlocks. He had very neat features and good grey eyes. His body was wiry and slim. He smoked Peter Stuyvesant and coughed. Peetie was from Tanganyika 'but forty years ago, medem'. He was a beautifully made little man. He looked like an older cherub carved from ebony, with even features and smiling eyes. He spoke in a formal way, smiled while he spoke, and was exquisitely well mannered.

What kept striking me was the positively courtly manners displayed by the older generation of farm labourers in the Valley. Nothing was ever too much trouble. Every meal or cup of tea was graciously accepted with thanks and a little dip of the head. Hats, even cloth caps, were removed in my presence until official greetings were over. Apollis, who worked for me on the top farm, used to sweep off his cap and go into a Regency bow. He had amazing blue eyes, broad shoulders, and a style that couldn't be improved upon at a royal court. He told me he had been sent to the Catholics in Malmesbury when he was five years old. He left when he was fifteen. They had given him a very good grounding.

I was enormously touched by the men's conduct towards me that morning. Martin was in charge, so I left them to it. They were to dig holes.

Spring had arrived. The earth was literally bursting with life. Millions of yellow oxalis were colouring the soil between rows of vines in my old vineyards, the big oak trees were in their first flush of new growth. It was a time when all the trees looked like salad, and succulent green covered every branch. All around Franschhoek the fruit trees were covered in pink or white blossoms. The plum trees growing along the wires, in their clouds of white like whipped cream, buzzed with millions of bees. The few birds there were whizzed around the clear sky chirruping and doing aerobatics. Some sort of delirium seemed to afflict the local people. Even the middle-aged became skittish, and relayed stories up and down the lines of trees about the scandalous seductions of the previous weekend.

Lyall Watson said in one of his books that human beings were merely the host for genes to replicate themselves in, and were impelled consciously or unconsciously to do so. If serious genetic observers researched Franschhoek in the spring, they would be convinced. Fertility hung in the air like a perfumed invitation. The people responded willingly.

Sometimes it was way beyond their control. Mothers of skinny schoolgirls, putting them to bed and smoothing the sheets over them, discovered buds of swollen flesh erupting upon their daughters' chests the next morning when they helped them into their school clothes. They were certain, quite certain, said the women, those breasts had not been there at bath-time the night before. Girls who were all angles and bones the previous summer grew rounded and heavy with juices, just like ripe fruit, and wore provocative expressions that made anxious fathers go and check out the family arsenal.

The boys had much more obvious problems. They might stand up to answer a question in front of the class, and a stranger's cracked voice would emerge from their throats, pitched either low or high; their own childish voice was gone forever. The choirmaster was desperate. How was he going to train new trebles in just three months, for the Christmas pageant? One unhelpful father reminded him that every year, when exuberant spring arrived, he had the same problem. Another father of five daughters suggested the ancient creation of castrati be reinstated. That would provide permanent singers for the choir, and solve the problem of the huge numbers of babies that seemed to hatch out in the Valley with an incubation period shorter than his chickens.

Tufts of hair that appeared upon an upper lip, under arms, or in more private places were an astonishment. How had it happened? When Ouma bathed the children last Saturday under the shower behind the house, they were not there! She knew, because the sun wasn't down yet and she would have seen it.

The consternation felt by all the parents was instinctual. The first menstrual blood of their daughters, and their animals, stirred fears about the mysterious nature of sexual life. The parents' thoughts were also mercantile. Young women as objects of marriage appraisal had to be inviolate, intact. Anything else had, in times past, given local men the painful feeling of having been defrauded and, moreover subjected them to the mockery of their friends.

Fortunately, sex education and closer relationships with parents have eased these subjects for all concerned, towards a more balanced and informed view of this physical leap into adulthood. Nonetheless, parents still rolled their eyes heavenwards. Help us, Lord, they prayed, here comes trouble.

❖

I took breakfast out at 10.30. We sat on rocks and discussed what to do next. The conversation was desultory. The two old men, Japie and Peetie, were so used to each other, they knew what the other had to say before he said it. I also discovered that Japie's principal entertainment was trying to find out if Peetie 'het iets gekry in die week'. Japie was married, and Peetie was not. His wife had died some years before. Japie's imagination was fired by his friend's single state. 'Sê my nou, het jy iets gekry?' he insisted.

'Ag, jy is vol kak,' replied Peetie in an amiable way, chewing happily on a chicken sandwich.

'What is it that you got this week, Peetie?' I asked in innocence. Martin guffawed loudly and swallowed half a sandwich, which went straight down his windpipe. We had to administer first aid, he was laughing so much. For me, the penny dropped.

Japie crowed. 'En wie was dit, wie het na die hoërskool meisies geloer in hulle gymnastic broekies toe hulle die oefeninge gedoen het laaste Vrydagmiddag?' He waited, in vain. 'Who was it who bought the new young teacher a Cadbury's chocolate bar also?' He fixed Peetie with a sharp eye. Peetie munched complacently on a hard-boiled egg, then slurped some coffee. He was smiling like Buddha.

Some women had arrived in the Dendy-Youngs' orchard next door. It was early season, and weeds had sprung up. Two of the younger ones had lifted their skirts and tucked them into their knickers so that their skirts would not snag in the weeds. Peetie was riveted by the sight. 'Kyk net daaie bene, jirre, 'n man wil net aan daaie bene vat, hulle is so mooi en so sag.' Oohh, he breathed out a sigh onto his fingers, almost like a kiss.

The girls were struggling to pull out a huge clump of khakibos. 'I think I go and help them, merrim,' said Peetie with a gleam in his eye, putting his plate and cup on the tray. Martin leapt to his feet and announced that breakfast was over, and the only place Peetie was going to was to carry the tray into the kitchen.

I asked Martin and the troops to dig some very deep holes for trees that I hoped would reach fifteen metres within ten years. I wanted to put a lot of nourishment in the holes.

My son Pete came up to the house some time later. He had chatted to Martin. Martin's comment about the depth of the holes was 'Fuck, Pete, next year I'll play rugby for the All Blacks. I'll be in New Zealand with this tunnel that your mother wants. Jislaaik, Pete, jou Ma hou nie op nie. And she still wants more holes for roses!'

I was always besotted with roses. In the most inhospitable soil of Rivonia, my mother contrived to have cascades of them all through the Highveld summers. The ground was grey and stony for the first twelve centimetres, then gave way to yellow- and ivory-coloured clay known as *ouklip*. When I first started digging in Franschhoek, I saw that the clays in which the vines and roses thrived looked just like that. No doubt the Rivonia farm's endless supply of chicken and cow manure played its part, because other than lime and bone meal there were no artificial fertilisers.

Mother's favourite rose was Charles Mallerin, whose deep crimson petals hid mysterious shadows of black. The perfume of this rose was the distillation of every lover's dream. But for me there was one rose Mother grew which I never saw anywhere else. She said its name was 'Paul ... something'. It was a strange pink before opening, the buds almost tube-like and easily seven centimetres long. When they opened their faces to the sun, the roses' full seductive beauty could be appreciated. Their size was that of a generous saucer, and their colour when just opened took on a different cast, like the skin-coloured celanese underwear Mother wore, turning after a few days in the burning Highveld sun to stains of mauve, like bruised flesh. I was watering this particular bush one afternoon, when I decided to count the blooms. There were 87 monster flowers on the bush, and to count them all I had to lean round and across the large bush, burying my face in the flowers time and again. They seemed to be exuding a putrifyingly sweet, unsettling smell – it was like my own newly flowing menstrual blood.

Ah, the lure of the disconcerting. Years later, Giuseppe Tomasi di Lampedusa flung me back through time to that hot, somnolent Highveld afternoon when I met this passage in *The Leopard*:

> It was a garden for the blind: a constant offence to the eyes, a pleasure strong if somewhat crude to the nose. The *Paul Neyron* roses, whose cuttings he had bought in Paris, had degenerated; first stimulated and then enfeebled by the

strong if languid pull of Sicilian earth, burnt by apocalyptic Julys, they changed into objects like flesh-coloured cabbages, obscene and distilling a dense almost indecent scent which no French horticulturist would have dared hope for. The Prince put one under his nose, and seemed to be sniffing the thigh of a dancer from the Opera. Bendicò, his dog, to whom it was also proffered, drew back in disgust and hurried off in search of healthier sensations amid dead lizards and manure.

These were the intriguing, memory-stirring roses I wished to grow in this southern garden, whose summers could certainly be similarly described.

Over weeks and months, the house and garden took shape. We took so many rocks out of the front slope that an eighty-metre wall was built with them. The Saturday morning gardening took on a special charm. The three faithfuls would arrive at 9 and, well fed at 10.30, would leave at 3 p.m. They provided me with all the village gossip from their community, and from mine.

New babies enchanted Peetie. Japie suggested that it was because half of them were Peetie's. 'Ag, hou op, Japie. If Peetie was so busy he wouldn't have time for work,' I said.

'Merrim,' Japie announced, 'my vriend het stemina!'

The gardeners provided a lightheartedness that I have never forgotten. I looked forward to their comfortable, amusing and obliging presence.

I had noticed some teasing of Martin, with the news that he now had a girlfriend. I asked about her. Yes, well, she was like pretty. She had done a Standard 8. She could cook – a man needed to check out these things, you know, merrim. And also, she would be getting a double bed from her Ouma. I said it was generous of Ouma. I was told Ouma didn't need the bed as she had died the previous month. Also, the girl believed in Jesus and attended Martin's church.

The very best was still to come. Thanks to a number of rugby-playing brothers, she could tell a fly-half from a full-back and she wouldn't mortally embarrass Martin if he took her to a rugby match. 'Some of the womens who come there, merrim, hulle is so onnosel! They shout for the full-back to score Own Goals! When you get to work on Monday, all the mens tell you that your wife is stupid. Women should not be allowed at rugby matches, finish en klaar!' She couldn't actually play rugby but, to compensate for this failing, she had an older brother who worked at the butcher in Wellington and could get meat at a discount.

I congratulated him on finding a girl with so many talents. Then I got down to business. 'Now Martin, is she pregnant?'

'Merrim, no, we don't do those things. She is a good girl. We will get married first in the church, and she has already her wedding dress. You know there is a lady in Groendal who sews very nice. You can come to the wedding, we invite you.'

'Martin, are you sure about this, because at the clinic they have a lot of information and condoms and the Pill. You need to save money for a little house before you start a family.'

I was assured that any such activity was way in the future.

Months later, there was still much to do, but in view of the tremendous effort by one and all, I suggested a little celebration. We would ask all the attendant relatives, to show off the men's handiwork. Now that's a lekker idea, they said in unison. The planning of the event was seized upon by Martin. After all, he went on trips all over the Boland with the rugby club. He would count the number of people for the number of bottles needed, and multiply by five. The bottles, not the people, he said. My experience with dinner parties in the Valley suggested that this was a well-established Franschhoek formula.

'What do you want to eat? Also how many children will be coming?' As I received overwhelming approval for my culinary efforts, the men left the menu to me. It would be hearty and plentiful. We reached a rough agreement on food, beverages and guests.

This last item had caused some discussion. 'Nee, nee, Kiepie kom nie!' Remember what he did last time! He drank too much, and after he had been *bos toe*, he forgot to pull up his zip! He only fastened the top button. He had walked full frontal into the gathering. Ouma, who was seated on the ground, had turned around to speak to her daughter, and right there, 'daar hang die ding'. She had such a *skrik*, her heart wasn't right for weeks.

There was much discussion of those who flirted, farted, fumbled with young girls, or otherwise disgraced themselves. Going over the alcohol limit was not punishable by exclusion. The guest list was closed. This was going to be a party with class. It was to show Merrim's new garden, and their handiwork was on display. Nothing was going to spoil their hours of glory!

A Saturday afternoon was chosen. The guests arrived in force before the appointed hour. The women, stylish and colourful, brought their high heels in plastic bags. That was very sensible, because there was a rough gravel road up to the house. I didn't recognise some of them. Lena had on a red satin turban, mascara, and vivid lipstick. A low-cut green blouse and tight skirt did justice to her full breasts, small waist and beautiful posture. She looked exotic, like someone who should be borne aloft by slaves. Other women were equally well turned out. Dinie wore a wonderful off-the-shoulder yellow blouse with a full white skirt. She had a good athletic body and looked ten years younger than she was. Make-up did the rest. Ouma was dignified in a blue dress, modestly cut, with a matching blue hat. On the hat she had an assortment of ragged feathers, which looked forlorn in spite of attempts to keep them at a rakish angle. They looked as if they had been plucked from some rather unwilling guinea fowl.

All the children were starched, scrubbed, beribboned, polished, and instructed to be on their best behaviour. This party was all about family pride. A compact man in a pinstriped suit arrived. He wore a pale blue shirt, cufflinks and a lovely striped tie. A Chicago-type fedora hat sat at a jaunty angle on his head. He carried a furled umbrella. It was Peetie. He looked like the President of Ghana, but his behaviour was considerably more gracious and diplomatic.

Once at the house, the ladies' high heels went on, for garden inspection. The Iceberg roses were doing their best, and small gardenia bushes were flowering. The instant lawn was installed and growing. A few spokes of lavender were visible. The small forest of trees was casting a bit of shadow. Cypresses formed a corridor down to the dam.

I told the guests of the heroic doings of the three men. Rocks the size of Mini Minors had been rolled off the site, just like that! With the smaller rocks, they built an entire wall. Pythons and other deadly *slange* were routed. Spiders the size of soup plates had been dispatched. In temperatures right up to 50 degrees, the men had laboured. In temperatures below freezing – well OK, not quite freezing – trees were planted, and roses, and hundreds of lavender plants. In the rain, hail and sleet they had stood firm! Martin's Ouma was quite damp-eyed. 'Ag siestog, my seuntjie,' she said, sniffing proudly. Her grandson had done all of that. 'My jinne, ag siestog!' I left out the diversions of watching the Dendy-Youngs' nubile pickers and the usual subject of tea-time conversations.

When all were suitably impressed, we got on with the main event, which was eating and drinking. It was most convivial, the company spread out on rugs on the lawn, children dashing about with the dogs, and the men conducting private tours to show off their work. I wondered, suddenly, which of the young women was Martin's girlfriend. I asked him where she was. 'Nay, merrim, sy voel nie goed vandag, she will come another day.'

'Oh, I am so sorry, Martin, this is your day today. She would have been so proud of you.'

Martin smiled his goofy smile. I looked at him closely. His head had shrunk. I remarked on it.

'Ja, merrim, ek het my hare gesny en gewas, I also washed my mussie.' Before you get the wrong idea, let me tell you that a *mussie* is a soft woollen pull-on cap. He continued: 'Now, merrim, is first time I can hear you.' He grinned at me. That explained just about everything!

Eight men were lounging about, glasses in hand, discussing the possibility of the Moorreesburg Rugby Club winning the Super Sevens. Two of them were involved in an argument of listless aggression, including a bit of familiar ridicule, about who was right, but they didn't have the energy to indulge in real anger. The others had heard Great News! There was a new wing who could run faster than the post office van through the Paarl Tunnel. 'But of course he can, stupid,' said Japie; 'for the van, there is a speed limit.'

The talk turned to weightier matters. Someone, deep in drink, had lashed out and embedded a knife in a friend's heart, killing him instantly. Remorse, most pitiful, could not sway the judges. 'Oh, goodness,' I said, 'what will happen?'

'Nee, merrim, hy sal swaai.'

'But what about an appeal?' I asked.

'Nee, hy sal swaai, piel en alles, merrim.' *Piel* is slang for penis.

At that moment a small figure ran panting into the middle of the festivities. 'Martin, Martin, jy moet huistoe, die baba kom,' he yelled. Martin looked at his feet, rubbed his nose.

'But whose baby is coming?' I asked him.

'It's my girlfriend, merrim, it is her baby,' he said.

'And who is the father, Martin?'

He looked at me expressionless. He sucked on his teeth, and a tear rolled down one cheek. 'Ek gaan 'n pa wees, Miz Gwen,' he said, giving way to the biggest smile he had ever smiled in his life.

He rushed down the hill to the little house, I swear beating the athletic rugby player, and was back again three minutes later.

'Merrim, kry jou kar *nou*, ons moet hospitaal toe. *Nou, nou.*'

I rushed into the house, found the keys, roared down the road, loaded up the hyperventilating mother and Martin. 'Martin, now listen to me! Are you listening? Don't let her push, for God's sake, *don't* let her push.' I was watching panic-stricken in the rear-view mirror. 'And also, what about not having sex, and birth control, and the wedding, and all that stuff?' I was nervous about the possibility of delivering the baby at the side of the road. 'Merrim,' Martin said, 'ons het besluit, ons gaan al daaie dinge doen ná die baba.'

By the grace of the gods who protect fools and imbeciles, we made it to Paarl Maternity Clinic. Martin sprang out, grabbed a wheelchair, and tenderly put his girlfriend into it. I was given the job of pushing the wheelchair, while Martin ran alongside holding her hand. Two Susters were waiting with the labour room's doors wide open. It was like roaring into a pit stop. Then the two starched, smiling and lovely ladies took over.

We went and sat in the waiting room together. Ten minutes later, one Suster came in, smiling widely. 'You have a son, hy is pragtig!' she said. Martin went to the labour ward to see his girlfriend and new son. I peeped through the window. The small family were all crying. We need a finely honed sense of cynicism, living in the Valley, but not so much that it keeps us from experiencing moments in our lives that come to us unexpectedly, joyful, whole and complete.

Later we drove home. The party was still in progress. Fresh supplies were found, and the little boy was toasted again and again. He was always the joy of Martin's life. His name was Peter, called after my youngest son, Martin's great friend. Not one day passed without talk of him, and I was told every detail of his achievements. I have never seen a prouder father than Martin.

The garden matured. Maybe we all did. I was in constant contact with the two older men, and Martin was the most faithful gardener. Whenever there was extra work, Japie and Peetie would come up the drive, smiling, cheerful and ready to help with anything.

I left Franschhoek years later, but always received calls at Christmas, or for my birthday, from the phone at the Franschhoek post office. I visited them often in Franschhoek, and they visited me in Constantia. It was always a happy time of 'Do you remember, merrim, do you remember when …' – then we all fell about laughing.

The very last occasion that I saw them was typical of the farce that seemed to befall us. They had not told me they were coming to visit. I was in my flat when the doorbell rang on the security gate. The intercom was fuzzy, so I went outside to look, having already pressed the gate release. Martin and Peetie were already marching down the drive. The door slammed behind me. I had not picked up my key, so we were now all locked out of the flat. We stood looking at the door, which wouldn't budge. Martin looked up and noticed that the upstairs study window over a balcony was open by an inch. 'Ek klim op, Miz Gwen,' he said, and in an instant he had swung himself up on a pergola, done a trapeze swing onto the balcony and was pulling on the window. Within two minutes he had wiggled it open. I gave him instructions on how to get down inside to the kitchen. The windows there were only on the latch. Martin duly appeared at the window and opened it.

I faced another problem. The window was high off the ground, and there was nothing to stand on. The men had a discussion. Martin, the dreadlocked Rasta, decided that if I leant a little forward he would grab my elbows; Peetie, the Tanganyikan, would 'stoot van agter'; and they could get me into the house. Fortunately I was wearing jeans, which are a uniform for me.

Martin was now lying across the kitchen counter, hanging out of the window, pulling me up, and Peetie was giving me muttered words of encouragement while getting a firm hold on my bum and pushing me up towards the window. A hard shove from behind got me hurtling through, pushing Martin onto the floor. He was still pulling on my arms, and I just missed falling on my head. I found the front door key, and Peetie made a more dignified entrance into the flat than I did.

Some reviving refreshments were called for, and we spent a happy afternoon getting up to date with the latest happenings in Franschhoek. I drove them down to the station. They were armed with some pocket money to keep them going, and I, waving casually to them going away in the train, didn't know that it was the last time I would ever see them.

There is a platitude that says one is incapable of appreciating a place in which one has spent but a short time. It's not true. It depends on the company you keep. I had kept company with people who had experienced and observed everything without judgement.

'Dis hoe die lewe is, merrim, ons kla nie,' they all said. They themselves have been the fabric of these valleys for three hundred and thirty years – not the newly arrived. Their families are all over the Boland, and they are as attached to it as any Afrikaner family, perhaps more so.

Some of them were born because of the seductive nature of the moonlit nights, the viticulture, and the ineradicable charm and strength of the women, many of whom still carry the genetic perfume of the East, from whence they had first made their graceful entrance into southern Africa. History tells us that their fine-boned fragility and petal-skinned fragrance were irresistible to the rough Northern men cast up in this harsh world, starved and lonely for the softness of women. The Eastern attitude of submission to male dominance, and acquiescence in pleasure, was a haven for these Calvinistic men. The pliancy, physical and emotional, of these sloe-eyed women served as a beguiling betrayer of reason and religion.

Postscript

I noticed that Martin did not phone for my birthday in 2002. Is it possible to have foreknowledge of a death? I already knew he was not with us. Later, in April 2003, I found that Martin had died the year before, at 38, of a brain aneurism. He leaves his only son, Peter, thirteen years old. Linkie, Martin's sister, has taken him as her child. Martin's wife, so carefully chosen, had made other plans three years before Martin died.

Peetie has also died, aged 74. Peetie's beloved daughter sat with him, holding his hand to the end as he made his preparations to leave. He passed gently into the spirit world, softly smiling, always willing to do whatever heavenly task was assigned to him.

I imagine them both in a field of pink and white blossoms. There will be a view of blue mountains, and the best red wine to drink. The Heavenly Choirs will be playing rugby against the Keepers of the Records. Peetie and Martin will have the best seats. They will be arguing about which of the angels is the prettiest, and which team will win the harp-playing competition this year. Of course it will be Western Province.

Japie lives with his wife and family in a house in Groendal which has been built for them by Dawn and Tom Darlington. Surrounding their house is a beautifully kept garden with white roses, lawns and hedges, lavender and cypress trees, and lots of spinach. Japie says that he often sees a small brown cherub sitting under the roses. Maria, his wife, says it is only on Saturday afternoons, when he has had some wine, quite a lot of wine, to drink, and he remembers with an aching heart the fine old times with his lifelong friend.

18

Franschhoek First Aid

Plans were drawn for our new house, builders found, and in late April work commenced. The rainy season starts in May. The conditions were not wonderful, but handymen were found from round about, friends and strangers arrived, and we went ahead.

Then winter really arrived, with the usual bouts of flu, running noses, bronchitis. There were also cuts, bruises, hangovers, fistfights and bumps on the head, but nothing serious. I got into the habit of having a first-aid roll call on a Friday morning. I wanted everyone medicated and taken to the doctor before the weekend.

On this particular Friday, the usual assortment of cough syrups, Disprins, gargles, Elastoplast and so on had been ordered and later dispensed. Some of the men were camping on the site in fairly primitive conditions. At three o'clock on the Friday afternoon, after receiving his pay, there remained a lone and isolated figure sitting on a boulder, a young and very thin man, a picture of misery. His usual honey colour had turned to a sallow yellow shaded with grey. He was clearly very unwell and depressed.

'Him is sick,' announced Andrew. Andrew, a tall black man, had appointed himself the major-domo and captain of the building crew.

'But I asked everyone this morning, Andrew. Why didn't he tell me?' I said. Andrew looked at his feet, cleared his throat and shuffled. 'Andrew, has he got a sexual disease?' I asked. I had been raised on a farm and understood the hesitancy of a man discussing anything of this nature with a woman.

'I think, merrim,' he said grudgingly.

'There is nothing I can do now, Andrew. The clinic is closed until Monday, the doctor is away for the weekend, otherwise he must go to Paarl Hospital. I will give him money for the taxi.'

There was a discussion. The hospital was not an option as far as this patient was concerned.

'Well, then, it's the clinic on Monday morning. I will take him at 8.30.'

The message was relayed. The wraithlike figure melted into one of the huts.

On Monday morning the boy – he was nineteen years of age, from Jo'burg – sat in silence next to me as we drove down the main road to the clinic. I looked at him out of the corner of my eye. His colour was awful, the teeth seemed to be pushing through his lips, the line of his limbs in the cheap clothing said that he was skin and bone. He was very ill.

The Franschhoek Clinic was housed on the side of the Town Hall. It was pandemonium. The weekend had produced its usual number of casualties. Black eyes, kneecaps kicked, bloody noses, ears half torn off, overexposure to the elements in states of undress, all sat along benches with incipient pneumonia, earache, suspected pregnancy and violent hangovers. The usual weekend wreckage.

The drill was that you checked in at a desk, stated your case if you were still in a condition to do so, then took your place clutching your roll-call number, sitting on a couple of benches in the middle of the room. You waited for Suster to call your number and tell you which cubicle you should go into to be examined, prodded, stitched or patched.

It was all very friendly. Babies were squalling, their mothers' breasts were uncovered to quieten them; gossip was exchanged, various beverages were shared, greetings and sympathies were loudly flung about the room, as were ongoing insults. Since almost everyone knew almost everyone else, it was like a rowdy family gathering. People farted or belched, men blew their noses into their fingers and wiped their fingers down their trouser legs. Comments about the weekend's activities were compared, and who did what to whom, and with what degree of success.

I wondered briefly how the former flower of the stockbroker set in Johannesburg had ended up in a place like this. I knew the answer. It was all by choice. We took our places on what looked like deconsecrated church benches and settled in to wait. The young man beside me seemed to shrink a little more.

The clinic was in the charge of Suster Betty Snyman. She was stiffly starched, in a gleaming white tunic; long dark hair tied into a bun, and an old-fashioned hardy face. Her eyes missed nothing, and she could hear unseemly suggestions being made at a hundred metres. She was built like a prop-forward, with decorations gained in medical service across a majestic bosom. You knew this one took no *kak*.

Nursing Suster Alice was in charge of maternity down the corridor. She had a face that suggested she could no longer be astonished. Quite clearly, she had experienced the wider shores of human aberration. Although no longer in the first flush of youth, she had a wiry body and breasts that bounced. Men spoke behind their hands, when she was consulting with a patient, of this alluring phenomenon. Her rooms were around the corner and five metres down the corridor. It wasn't a long corridor, and closing her door was not high on her list of priorities when you would just have to open it again. Privacy was not highly regarded.

Suster Petra, still young and sweet, was in charge of quick solutions. Her mother had taught her needlework, so stitching bits of anatomy back on was her speciality. She also removed foreign objects from whichever orifice they had been secreted in, and attended nappy rashes, small burns and *so voorts*. The patients loved her, with her wide smile and nice green eyes.

First call after we settled in was a slip of a girl, fine-boned and graceful, with a toddler on her lap. She walked down the corridor after Suster Alice. No door was banged shut. The audience drew a collective breath of anticipation. 'Bly still, almal,' hissed a voice, 'ons wil alles hoor.' The shuffling ceased, babies were hushed.

'Vat af jou broekies,' we all heard, 'maak oop jou bene, ek moet 'n vinger insteek.' There was silence, the audience straining to hear. 'O God,' boomed Suster Alice, 'nou is nommer drie op pad. Kan jy en jou man nie 'n boek lees, of het julle nie 'n TV om na te kyk nie?'

There was a reflective pause, then the girl replied, 'Maar jy sien, hy was *so-o-o-o* lank weg om vis te vang, en ek het so vir hom verlang.'

'Maar moet jy so vir hom verlang?' boomed Suster Alice. The question hung in the air above us.

Just at that moment we were diverted by Suster Betty laying a meaty *klap* against someone's ear. 'Waar sit jy jou hande, onnosel, wil jy vrek?' she asked in a threatening voice. I wondered if it was dignity or her laundry which concerned her. The onnosel had left a grubby mark on her pristine white bosom. He hung his head, bleary and unkempt, and tried to salvage his dignity.

'Maar Betty, ons het altyd gevry, as jou Ma in die kombuis was …' He was not allowed to finish the sentence.

'Uit hier,' she bellowed, pushing him out of the door and down the steps, where he sat crumpled but indignant.

People came and went, and we heard most of the diagnoses and much that we shouldn't have. Since a lot of the patients were related or worked together, they didn't seem to mind. The young man with me clearly did. He was sweating mildly and hanging on to my elbow like a child. I understood his agitation and got up to speak to Suster.

'You know, Suster, the young man I have brought here is not one of the locals and he is very shy: can you please close the door when you examine him?'

'Oh, of course, merrim, don't worry at all,' she said.

Thus reassured, I went and sat down again. Finally our number was called. I nudged the boy. He hesitated and looked at me pleadingly. I shook my head and told him to follow Suster. She closed the door, so the preliminaries were muted. The audience looked at me accusingly as if I had spoiled their fun. It was like missing an episode of *Dallas*. A few minutes passed.

Suddenly the door was wrenched open, and Suster in full voice yelled, 'Suster Alice, kom kyk gou hier!' The urgency in her voice brought Alice sprinting up the corridor. The breasts bounced to unanimous male approval. The door slammed behind her. Two minutes later it was Suster Alice yelling for Suster Petra, who obliged on the trot, and the door slammed shut again.

The audience, denied their news, concluded that I could shed some light on the goings-on. I returned their stares and shrugged shoulders. I should have known better. It was Suster Snyman at the open door. 'Merrim, please come and look here.' I got to my feet and followed her into the room. I didn't dare look round.

He lay pallid and sweating against the sheet. His trousers were off and legs apart. His misery was palpable. Tears rolled down from the outer corner of his eyes and puddled into his ears. He was also shivering. Four women looked at a particular part of his anatomy.

'Look, merrim,' said Suster. I looked very carefully. A hole was rotted diagonally across the shaft of his penis. The foreskin was full of eruptions and inflammation. The testes were lumpy and bruised-looking. Discoloration was spreading across his groin. I could not look into his eyes. I did not want to see what he already knew.

'Did he have underwear?' I asked. No, he didn't. The rough trousers scraping against the open wounds must have been an unbearable pain.

I gave it some thought. *Eureka!* Inspiration had struck.

'Suster,' I said, 'do you have any condoms?'

'*Jirre*, merrim,' she looked shocked. 'He is not thinking about sex in his condition.'

I explained that if there was some soothing cream against the wound, inside a condom, it would certainly give him some relief until I could get to the Co-op and buy him some underpants. Then I would take him to the Paarl Hospital.

'Ja, now that's a bloody good idea.' It got a nod from the starched triplets.

I left the waiting room, shortly followed by the young man, now dressed. He didn't ask, just put his arm through mine and hung on to me. The audience was baffled. What was going on? Both the young man and I gazed vacantly at the notice board.

'Just wait here a moment, merrim,' said Suster, going down to the dispensary. She returned minutes later. She dumped two dozen packets of condoms and two tubes of KY jelly into my arms, turned around, and called out the next number. We were dismissed.

I walked out of the clinic and down the steps, condoms dropping to the floor and the young man firmly hanging on to my arm. After bending to rescue another packet, I looked up. In front of me stood a man. Not just any man, but Grant Fear, linguist, international traveller, immensely sophisticated European diplomat, an old Africa hand for the UN, and close personal friend. He was smiling like the proverbial cat. He had taken in the scene and my embarrassment at a glance.

'O Lord,' I said, 'not you here!'

'Bill still in Johannesburg I take it, Gwen?' he said in his beautifully cultivated accent that seems to be the birthright of properly educated Englishmen. 'It's been a long time. When is he finally coming back?'

I ran to the car without reply. I knew that his capacity for storytelling would not be able to resist a story such as this.

First stop down the main road was Johnny Bell, the chemist. 'Could we talk in private?' I ask.

'Sure, come into the office,' says Johnny.

I didn't think an over-the-counter description of what I had just seen would go down well in Johnny's crowded shop. It might put the delicately reared matrons off their morning tea and scones. I described what I'd just seen in detail, and told him that the patient was now in my car.

'I'm not sure, Gwen, but it sounds like advanced syphilis. Give him money and get him into a taxi immediately. They will drop him off at Paarl Casualty. I have only once or twice in my career seen what you are describing.'

'Thanks, Johnny,' I said.

We drove up the hill in a dense and strained silence, for we both had knowledge of what was to come. He went inside one of the temporary houses, collected his few things, then I drove him down to the taxis and handed him some money.

He never spoke but looked at me briefly in acknowledgement, as a stray dog would look, having received a crust from a stranger. Then he was out of the car and into a departing taxi. He had come to us impaired, and then been blown away like an autumn leaf in the wind. Andrew never asked about him again.

19

House Guests

A large house in the country containing several guest rooms acts as a magnet, particularly in the Boland. The phone rings on a Monday evening. The usual pleasantries are followed by prolonged verbal foot-shuffling. 'We just thought we might stop over in Franschhoek after the trip to Hermanus. Just one night when it's not inconvenient? I know you will just let us get on, so we won't be in the way.'

My mother started the rot. The farm in Rivonia was home and haven to any of the large numbers of relatives with whom she stayed in contact. Our house was occupied intermittently by relatives from Cape Town, Pretoria, Durban, England – or Ireland, as once happened, with parents and three children, one of them aged six months. They stayed for several months. My sister and I would be rehoused in the porch, a small room off the sitting-room. Any opposition from two belligerent daughters was not tolerated by my mother, as this was deemed the only civilised way to treat family.

With so much food on the farm, the immediate economics didn't seem to matter. The bounty of the vegetable and fruit gardens, abundant milk, yogurt, cream, cream cheese, eggs, chickens, breads, scones, jams, bottled fruits and vegetables, home-made ginger beer, and fruit syrups of every variety ensured that no one ever went hungry.

In my own home in Johannesburg, with three gregarious boys and lots of space, the same thing happened. Boys who were 'coming to play' turned up as bodies at the breakfast table, and we might have more visitors than there were packets of muesli or lunchboxes packed. Having guests is part of my life, and my sister is similarly afflicted.

My very first guest in Franschhoek was Sarie, my cousin from Pretoria, who is a botanist and my favourite companion above all others. Her particular study is liverworts, and together with mosses the group is called bryophytes. By happy chance she had been asked to contribute an illustrated article on bryophytes to a popular magazine. In Pretoria in midwinter, the likelihood of finding living material was remote, so a trip down to the Boland offered opportunities for a longed-for family visit and some collecting of living material. I thought she should take a look, or at least be interested to see where we were. She arrived a week later.

It was not really weather for field trips. All through that June and July it continued raining, and, seeing my first Cape winter, I thought it would never stop. Mosses were growing along the Pass Road above the farm. I had never seen such a thing. The more shaded parts of the Pass Road at the first big bend looked like lawn and was that gorgeous green that makes one think of Wimbledon, English summer and strawberries.

Still, since the fruit season was at a lull, we set off each day armed with brown paper bags, waterproof ink pens, small absorbent papers, magnifying glasses, a spatula or penknife – all the tools of her trade, plus a card from the Botanical Institute authorising her to collect samples. As we drove along, she tried to describe what she might look for, and the differences between liverworts and mosses.

We were driving along towards Robertsvlei when I was directed to stop. There was a likely-looking donga! We were wearing our imported fluffy-lined Israeli War Surplus gumboots, at twenty rands a pair, waterproofs, jumpers and jackets, and waterproof hats. It hadn't stopped raining yet. There was snow about, and there was really no point in getting frozen.

We got into the ditch and bent low to see what might be there. 'Gwennie, look at this, it's a find,' she cooed. 'This is a female.'

'How can you tell?' I asked. 'And how does the male get from where he is stuck on a rock to the bottom of this ditch when the moon is full or something, and does he phone first or just drop in?'

'Well, it's not quite like that,' she said, and went on to an elementary lecture on botanical reproduction. She is the most marvellous companion. She has a wide-ranging and acute intelligence, and is never dictatorial, having a fine sense of the ridiculous, and she laughs easily. A good teacher and friend indeed.

We spent happy days along the Berg River, walked miles up the waterworks roads and, later, from the top of the Pass Road, we walked cross-country to Wemmershoek Dam.

The countryside was lush and slippery from the torrents of rain. Sarie kept up a botanical commentary on everything we saw. Later, other trips were made towards Hermanus and back to Worcester. Evening conversations, after warmth and food, were of family history, our children, science, books and more books, music, medicine, great movies, and events in our lives which were intertwined, our mothers being sisters.

One day, after driving and walking long distances, we stopped at the Houw Hoek Inn. We settled into comfortable chairs and had a most pleasant lunch on the veranda. I looked across the courtyard to the fountain. In the centre of the fountain sat a cherub holding an urn, from which water flowed. What did I see but a large circle of moss growing on the cherub's backside. Oh, what a find!

One of the conventions regarding collecting is that one marks the label accompanying the specimens to record exactly where the samples were taken: '5 km from crossroads' and any other pointers such as road signs, trees, doorways, fences or walls. If it is an important collection, explicit instructions and accuracy as to location are vital. Another necessity is that the collector leaves enough of the plant material to replicate itself, to be there for future researchers.

I called her over to the fountain. 'Sarie, you have to look at this. I'd like the Institute's records to catalogue the cherub's *gluteus maximus*, or call it his arse.' But she was not falling for any nonsense. We found enough of interest to justify the trip, and the article she wrote was very well received, without mention of cherubs. I learnt several botanical facts, which I have now forgotten, but the memory of the splendid time we had together I shall always treasure.

❖

After selling the farm and spending months renting the manor house at Chamonix, we finally moved into our half-completed house. It was 20 December 1990. In the next few days we tried to get things in some order. Dinie and her sisters, Juna and Paulina, were roped in to help.

The first priority was cleaning the house from top to bottom, as the builders had left two days before and it was filthy. Then we unpacked some crockery, cutlery, linen, pots and pans, wine and a hundred cases of books (I had my priorities). Clothing was hung up in the dressing-room. I could at last find things – we had been living out of baskets and boxes for four months. We took a deep breath and relaxed.

We had guests for Christmas Eve. They were very dear friends. I showed them to their bedrooms. Annette checked out their bathroom. She came into the kitchen looking worried. 'Gwennie, dear, there doesn't seem to be a window in the bathroom. Are you sure that nothing will climb in here during the night? By the way, what is that ladder doing in the entrance hall?'

'There is no window in the bathroom, Nette. I have no idea who or what might come through the window. Lock the bathroom door at night. The ladder is what I climb several times a day to get upstairs to my bedroom, because the carpenter hasn't been seen for months. We do have the finished staircase standing in the garage, which is why we park outside. I have a sink with a bucket underneath instead of pipes. I have not seen a movie for six months. I haven't had a haircut for six months, or a manicure or anything that might make me feel human. We have six sheets, six towels, and probably no soap. I managed to find your pillows this morning. The rest of my worldy goods are in two different garages. But we have lots of wine and lots and lots of food.' Eating had become a refuge during the last few months.

She looked at me. 'I do think that you are a little tired, darling. It has been so exhausting for you. Why don't you sit down and let Archie pour you a nice little drink.'

A drink, any drink, tasted better by the day. But sleep was what I craved. Archie poured me the nice little drink, which I drank in one gulp. He poured me another very nice little drink and announced he was going to shower before supper. Annette, John, Bill and I sat on the veranda and chatted. It was lovely to be hospitable again. We hadn't been able to have friends around for six months.

This pleasant, contemplative mood was shattered by horrible screeches and some fairly fruity cussing. 'That sounds like Archie,' said his beloved. Indeed it did.

'Which cretinous idiot son of a bitch was your plumber, Gwen? Couldn't the bastard tell that Red is for hot and Blue is for cold? I would like to subject him to what I have just endured, the shit!'

Archie had turned on the cold tap to be invigorated after the long hot journey. He left it running while he collected a towel and fresh underwear, then stepped under a gushing flow of scalding water.

'I would like to get hold of the fucker and separate him from his balls. May he rot in hell!'

This flow of invective was interrupted by Annette saying, 'It's all right, darling. Gwennie has some burn cream, and I will inspect you and see where to rub it on.' Somewhat mollified by this attention, he calmed down. Well, no doubt about it, our hospitality was off to a rather rickety start.

❖

Weekends came and went, and the house gradually became more user-friendly. The bathroom got its window and the taps were exchanged. No further cases of burn damage were reported. The staircase was installed in late February. Curtains arrived in March.

Proper plumbing was installed under the sink, and Valerie's beautifully hand-crafted tiles, specially ordered, were fitted onto the kitchen walls. And more than that. I came home from a day in Cape Town. The entire house was decorated with wonderful Persian carpets – or, I should say, additional wonderful carpets. O God, Bill had gone mad, a buying spree had overtaken him. But no, it was John Benjy, who had arrived to stay for the antique dealers' fair, to be held in Franschhoek that year

The stream of visitors were reassured. Deeply reassured! I was obliged to take bookings for weekends.

One visitor arrived from England, but he was spending only three weeks and was willing to help us finish the house. He was an engineer, and a perfectionist – oh, thank God for him. He did do an enormous amount of work for his board and lodging. I got so used to him that it was only after some thought that I realised he had been with us for four months. He was a fixture at the local pub too.

I mentioned it to Bill on one of his infrequent visits from Johannesburg.

'Yes, well, I suppose he had better leave.'

'You will have to tell him,' I said. 'After all, he is your brother.'

It was another two months before he left, most regretfully. The bar's profits took a serious dip.

A lifelong friend from England who is a passionate and inventive cook came to stay for a month or so. Cookbooks were dragged out and we sat for hours reminiscing of meals eaten and cooked in England and Spain, where I had worked for a year and she had come to stay with me for some time. Insanity desires company to sample and savour all the promised culinary delights, so a few phone calls gathered up like-minded companions.

On the morning of the lunch a Spanish friend visiting from Johannesburg asked if she could join us. Of course she could. But she said she had a friend with her. 'Isobel, bring the friend, I will be delighted.'

'But you see, Wendolina [there are no 'gw' sounds in Spanish; working in Spain I got used to being called 'When'!], he is from the Church.' Her father had been the Spanish ambassador to the Vatican and to America in the Kennedy era. Catholic dignitaries appeared from time to time.

'Well, fine, he eats, doesn't he?'

The guests arrived, greetings were exchanged, and bottles were opened. The guest from Rome had to be explained to the kitchen staff.

'Merrim,' said Dinie, 'why is that man wearing a dress? It is such a *vrot* colour, but I wouldn't mind wearing his rings.'

'Mind your own business, Dinie,' I said.

The visitor was erudite, urbane, worldly and fond of good food. He had lived in several continents, and was both interesting and interested in different cuisines.

After the meal the London chef was explaining how she had cooked the delicious whole *stompneus*, a fish of the waters around the Cape coast. It was a dish approaching poetry, having been wrapped in leeks and the finest slivers of fennel, and then basted, with the perfume of aquavit and garlic.

'What about avocados as a wrapping?' one guest asked.

'Oh, no, no, no,' said the chef firmly.

'Why not?' insisted the guest. 'Would it spoil the avos?'

'No,' said a voice firmly from the end of the table, 'it's the fish that will be fucked.'

I slid straight under the table on the pretext of finding my napkin. I was overtaken by a horror of the priest being offended. I listened carefully, and all was well. Confessionals must yield a wide spectrum of human fallibility including robust sexual talk and cussing.

As I crawled back onto my chair, I thought I saw a muffled smile in the corner of his mouth. He raised a glass in salutation to the cook.

I went into the kitchen. By the time I came out, bearing the coffee tray, decorum had been restored.

'What poise and intelligence that lovely man had,' said the London chef. 'Great pity the Church got him before I did.'

The couple from Brussels, Bill assured me, were used to Only the Very Best. He chaired a global financial company, and they would be staying with us for four days.

'And his wife,' I asked, 'what is she like?'

'Uhm … I don't think he is bringing his wife.'

'Well, is it his mistress, or what?'

'I think it's, um, What,' said Bill.

They arrived from the airport in a limousine. He was portly, gracious, and as sleek as a tiger. One knew he was nourished on expense-account lunches and dinners at three-star restaurants. Clearly he was a tycoon, in late middle age, and he wore his tailor-made clothes well. A massive Rolex, which appeared to tell the time on four different continents and the share prices in New York, Frankfurt and London, weighed down his wrist.

Her Rolex was studded with diamonds. She was every wife's dream of disaster. She clung, and so did her clothing. She was a tall girl, early twenties, good long legs, bored eyes, sharp cheekbones and heavy blonde hair, with a dissatisfied sexy mouth.

She walked over to me slowly. 'What time is dinner?' she asked, without introducing herself. 'You may call us at seven, we will now go to rest.'

'Bill, what the hell is this? Did you tell them that I was employed to run a guest house? I was not wearing a uniform or an apron, and I managed not to curtsy!' I was furious.

'Look, she is spoilt. I don't think she meant to treat you like the housekeeper,' said Bill.

'Well she did, and I am pissed off.'

Supper was three hours away, and all the preparations were complete. Dinie was in the kitchen preparing the salad ingredients. I had time to spend, so I spent it on myself.

We were sitting in the library when they joined us. We had four other guests already sampling the Boland's latest, best champagne. My hair was washed, face immaculate, nails manicured, and I'd made the most of my bosom: it was cantilevered and exposed, since I had put on a black lace push-up bra and left most of the buttons down the front of a new red silk shirt unbuttoned.

'Good God,' said Bill when I had come down the stairs. He seemed incapable of saying much more.

The chairperson was not looking rested, quite the contrary. He might have spent the entire afternoon on a trampoline. To my satisfaction, he appeared to be mesmerised by my bosom.

I could write a book about the politics of table placement. The tycoon sat at my right hand, the young lady was placed far away, at the other end of the table, next to Bill. She was the youngest by many years and this time it didn't do her any good. The evening was filled with excellent conversation, reminiscences, friendships, and intellectual love affairs. Journeys were discussed; there were ones undertaken to remote places, visited before she was born.

History and politics she knew nothing of. She had her function in life, but nothing to contribute to the conversations raging round the table. The dinner was outstanding, one of those memorable meals, as perfect as I had planned it to be.

It didn't surprise me at all when they announced after lunch the following day that they would be going back to Cape Town. She had already ordered the limousine, which would arrive within the hour. I waved them goodbye.

'That wasn't nice,' said Bill. I gave him one of those looks. It wasn't worth a reply.

❖

Frank and Maggie were old friends, and experienced ornithologists. They had a farm in the Magaliesberg, north of Johannesburg, which was home to over three hundred bird species. They were in the Cape to do research, mapping Western Cape birds, and their luggage when unpacked consisted mainly of large data books, binoculars, telescopes, nets, rings and other paraphernalia. Clothing was in one small carry-bag each.

They invited me to go out with them one morning. 'Gwen, I think you should drive, then I can tell you where to stop when I see something interesting,' Frank said. That was fine by me: I like driving.

Frank was an Anglo-Dutch mixture. He was sturdy with a paunch, weather-beaten and jocular. He loved food and wine, and swore in colourful blasts of language. If Maggie were a bird, she would be a turtledove. She had been an accountant, and a very successful one, and it was in the large listed company where she worked that she had met Frank, a fellow accountant. He was married at the time and so was she.

This was a second marriage for both of them. They were so happy, I just had to ask her how they had got together. They had been working together for some time with other accountants on very large investment projects. They hardly spoke to one another and were always surrounded by colleagues. One Saturday at lunchtime, Frank arrived at the apartment shared by Maggie and her husband. He walked in, greeted Maggie's husband, and told her to pack her things as she was coming to live with him. She was so astonished, the first thing that came into her head was the immediate practicality. 'But I am just cooking some fillet steak for lunch,' she said. Frank told her to eat her lunch with her husband and then pack her things; which she did, chewing each bite for a long time so that she could work out what to take and what to leave, while both men watched her without speaking – her husband from across the table and Frank leaning nonchalantly against the dining-room wall, staring fixedly at her. She said she felt as if she had been struck by an earthquake, but she never doubted she should follow Frank's lead.

I had driven Frank as my binoculated passenger before, in Spain. His shrieks still sounded in my ears: 'Sto-o-o-o-op left (or right)! There is a rare owl, just on that fence. Damn it, Gwen, I told you to stop! The owl has now gone. Damn, damn, damn!' – all this regardless of thirty-ton olive-oil trucks bearing down on us from behind.

Warily, I climbed into the driver's seat of their large Jeep. Off we went, over the pass and along to Hermanus. Frank was looking for any signs of vultures or eagles. Away in the distance there was some activity, but it was all fenced off and we couldn't get close. For once, we'd have a relatively calm drive! A couple of hours later, we went back towards Stellenbosch and ended up near a large dam at Elsenburg, the budding winemakers' college. Oh, that was better, all sorts of feathered things were on the dam and in the air. We spent a happy day, ate our picnic lunch, and finally headed for home.

Compared with the Transvaal, Frank told me, the Cape has pitifully few birds. Certainly Franschhoek was almost devoid of anything that flew. They had all died because of the huge quantity of poisons sprayed in the Valley at the time. Sitting drinking some wine later under the trees in the garden, Frank and Maggie told me that they would not be out the next day, and would have a late morning.

It happened to be the strawberry season. After supper I hulled twenty kilos of fruit, weighed it and added sugar, to marinate overnight. Strawberry jam was a favourite in the house. The next morning I did my usual rounds of the farm. Then, since I could hear they were awake, I asked our guests if they would like some tea.

I brought the tea in their room and we talked happily for a long time. We really had so much to catch up on. At one stage Frank went off to make a telephone call, and came back. An hour passed, and I was suddenly aware of something burning. What could it be?

I turned into the corridor towards the kitchen, which was smoke-filled. I ran down and found myself sticking to the floor. I got into the kitchen and saw that the four huge pots were on the stove, glued to it, with red froth like a volcanic eruption running over the rims of the pots, down the stove, and making its way along the floor and down the corridor.

A cook I admire, Arabella Boxer, in a piece published in *Vogue*, said, '*Never* turn your back on strawberry jam.' I could see what she meant.

'Oh, my God,' said Frank behind me, 'I forgot that I switched on the stove. Oh, I am so sorry, Gwen.'

I had not switched on the stove for the jam to cook, but Frank had when he had finished his phone call, and then he had forgotten. All the stove plates were on High, and the top of the stove was smouldering. Smoke filled the kitchen and most of the other rooms. From outside, it looked to the arriving staff as if the entire house was on fire. Dinie ran into the kitchen screaming, with a bucket of water in her hands. I had to explain what had happened.

Two hours later, when the stove had cooled, we began to chop the pots loose. Scouring pads were bought, and Vim and paint thinners, to remove the burnt sugar off the enamel of the stove and off the wooden floor. By suppertime we had cleaned up most of the mess. Strawberries were not on the menu.

'Well, you know, Gwen,' said Frank, 'I do make jam commercially. I am so used to it, I must have thought I was at home.'

Besides the inconvenience, what better accolade could a hostess have?

20

Rooi Jan Boonzaaier's Story

It is Saturday afternoon, and I am sitting with Anna-Marie Burger, the curator of the Franschhoek Museum. We are thinking out loud about people I might still get stories from, to fill out the background of the earlier days in Franschhoek. She suggests that I go up the hill towards Swiss Farm, and just on the bend I will find a small cottage on the right-hand side of the road, and if I drive in I can ask for Rooi Jan Boonzaaier.

I do exactly that, and find myself at a modest cottage. In the yard is a small girl pushing a pram in which sits a wide-eyed doll with curly brown hair. The child herself is dressed in tiny green shorts and a fitted pink T-shirt, and has two little pigtails tied with pink ribbons. She looks at me with no interest until I speak to her.

It is 4.30 in the afternoon. 'Middag, meisie, is Rooi Jan hier?' I ask her. 'Ja,' she says. I ask if I may speak to him. She does not reply, but nods, and pushes the pram round the far end of the cottage. Perhaps two minutes later, a man follows her back round the corner of the house.

Jan is no longer young; in fact he tells me later that he is 79 years old. What I see is an immaculate, fine-looking man, white T-shirt with collar and cuffs pressed and spotless, sharply pressed beige trousers, a good belt, and gleaming polished shoes. He comes to me smiling and holds out his hand.

I tell him the purpose of my visit and he modestly says that what he has to say is not very interesting. We sit on a slatted bench facing down the Valley. Under my coaxing he tells me this story.

❖

My father was not very healthy. He was not very well in his head, and he moved from job to job. He could not work long anywhere. When I could remember, we went to live at the Haumanns' behind the station. Then my mother went to work in Paarl, and I lived with my uncle and aunt in Groendal or I lived with Mr Malherbe at La Dauphine. My father had a lot of health problems, I think he was epileptic, and then my mother left him.

I lived with my mother and a brother and two sisters. We played with everyone. All the children used to get together and play the *outydse speletjies* like *blik-aspaai*, marbles, *bok-bok*, *Jan Blou*. It didn't matter if you were white or coloured, we all got on very well. When we got older, my brother Dirk and I played rugby very seriously. We practised a lot, and played club rugby. He belonged to a Paarl club called Mountain Rocks, and they were tough, I tell you. He started to get sick in his early twenties and couldn't play any more. But I went on and even played a few games at provincial level. Our colours were blue and white.

Time went by and we grew up, but at that time Franschhoek was no longer a nice place. We had all lived in the village, if not on the farms, or in houses in Le Rouxville and Groendal. There were many coloured children at the Franschhoek school, and nobody cared. Coloureds and whites lived side by side in the village houses and used to be good neighbours and respect each other. We sat next to each other at church, and I was on the church council for years. The women used to *kuier* with each other, and the men used to have a drink together, while the children would play together in each other's gardens.

Then Dr Verwoerd came to power and all our lives changed. Apartheid had come with Dr Verwoerd. Then all the terribleness began. If we walked in the street with our white friends, the young Afrikaans policemen used to get their motorcycles up on the pavement and drive slowly along next to us and say, 'You Hottentots, what are you doing here? You can't walk on the white man's pavement,' and they told us we must get out of the village. Then they would get out their sjamboks and start to hit us across our shoulders and legs. I thought at first it was some horrible joke that would stop but it didn't stop; it got worse and worse.

[In the fading afternoon light Jan looks away from me. He is unable to go on for some time. Then he speaks again.]

Afterwards I began to get a little understanding, and then the apartheid stories started. I could never understand what was going on. We had all lived together and carried on with our lives and we hadn't changed. Now we had to leave the village and go and live on a farm or in the 'coloured area'. I remember some of the wonderful Afrikaans neighbours sitting with us crying in the house, and apologising for this terrible thing that was happening. But they could not help us. It was the government. Before that time, it was a good place and everyone was friendly and we all respected each other. The coloured and the white people used to live in town in houses side by side, and were good neighbours.

I had got my Standard 3, and I loved History and I got good marks for it. I used to read English books and I read about Dingaan. At the white school there was a teacher called Miss Reineke, and her father was a Dominee at the Congregational church. They were both so very kind to us. Also Mr Malherbe at La Dauphine, and the Maskies at Swiss Farm, they were such good people.

My mother worked in the village. She worked for a Mrs Herbert. Her husband was an engine driver who took the trains out of Beaufort West. She saw that I liked reading and so she always gave my mother books for me to read. I eventually moved to the bottom of the village, and there was a clump of houses there and a farm called Vrede. Mr Siebrits, he was the Dutch Reformed *Sending* Church Dominee. He was our Dominee also and so we went to that church. He was born a year before me, and now he is already dead.

The years went on with apartheid. Then one day I went to my church, and suddenly we had a white *leraar*, his name was Coetzee. One Sunday, it was in 1965, he says to us that we must make way for the white people. I was on the church council for years, but he says we cannot be any longer, and we must move away out of the town, and the Congregational church must go also. I asked him then, Where must we go to church?, and he said we must go somewhere else. This went on and on and there was a meeting in the Town Hall, and everyone was very cross and shouting, they said the church can just stand empty. We tried to talk over the years, but there the church still stands.

We had to leave the village then, and we moved to a farm called Burgundy. The owner was Dawid le Roux's father, and there beside the road was the rest of the family all living close together. Then Champagne got Mr Sven, who married Miss Fay, and then some English people started to come to the Valley.

We were only farm workers, and not allowed to own land, so our children left and went to work and live elsewhere. Quite a number of them work at the Pinelands City Lodge. Even my daughters work there, and they have their own houses nearby, where they live. My own son, the one that is sick now, he has also gone away to the Kaap, to Cape Town, to work. Later my other son came back and he is the foreman on a farm now – there were other people who bought the farm from Nick Norman, and my son worked for them. He now lives in Groendal.

I had my own cows and sheep, not a lot, but I loved the animals. They all had names, and they would come when I called them.

We became firm members of the Dutch Reformed *Sending* church, in Dirkie Uys Street. There was also the Congregational church, and we were all together, the farmers and us, but it didn't work. They didn't want to be in the church with the *plaasjapies*. So they went back to their own Congregational church and they separated it. But we stayed with the church and we still go to this day.

At Christmas time my mother bought sweets and little cars for us, but the big thing was the Christmas choirs. My brother-in-law and my uncle used to practise for months, and so I would hear all the lovely songs like 'Bethlehem Star' and 'Silent Night'. And we would go and sing all the way up and down the Valley, and it just felt special. It was a time I loved.

Getting leave from work, after the harvest? We didn't get much, three days over a weekend – some got nothing. But we would put our money together, all hire a bus and go for one day to the beach. To see the sea was like the very best present, and you looked for that day for the whole year, it was so wonderful.

Did I get interested in girls when I grew up? Ja, well, people did look and see if there was one. But the one I liked was living in the Kaap, in Cape Town, and she married a man from George. Her sister married a white man in the Cape Town municipality and they went to live in England. I had very good friends among women. Mary May's sister, she was so beautiful, and she is married to a German, and she lives in Germany.

My grandmother was quite dark in colour. Her first husband died young. My surname is Boonzaaier. But if I go on my correct name, it should be Hendriks. My name was meant to be Willem, but I was called Jan by mistake. My father was a white man's son. The coloured women were very attractive and loving, and the white men liked them very much. That stuff is not finished yet –

the white men still like the coloured women. I got to know other white men who didn't like coloured men at all but who loved to *vry* the coloured girls and made more coloured children with them. My mother and her sister both had children before they were married. It happened a lot and nobody said anything.

Ag, that tot system. As a young child you got some wine. It was very cold in winter, and we didn't dress very warm, so some men would come from the farms with bottles and pour the children wine: they said it made you warm. They came before school and then at the break time. And then also after school they would be waiting for us. The teachers told them to get away but they kept coming. And so by the time you were fourteen, fifteen, you were already an alcoholic, and you had to have that wine. And they gave free cigarettes also. Men got sick because of all the smoking and drinking, and died, because we were all poor and didn't get enough food, and we had all that free wine and cigarettes – it stopped your hunger. All over the Boland, men died. You got bad stomach pains and stomach cancer, and your lungs gave in. And you got TB.

It was terrible for the families. A woman would watch her husband and her sons die. Most of the women did not drink. I think they wanted to be there for their families, and they worked all their lives.

When you started work, the first thing was a mug of wine. Then 8 a.m., 11 a.m., lunchtime, then three times more in the afternoon, and some to take home. I used to get terrible stomach cramps – it was not good wine. I went to the doctor and he said that if I didn't stop, I would die of stomach cancer. So I stopped. A lot of people saw that I stopped and tried to make me start again. But I didn't want to die, and I prayed to the Lord, and I believe he helped me. God had to look after us in this Valley.

Jan is all talked out. We sit in silence for a while. The sun has gone down behind us. He is a beautiful man, not embittered by the past, calm, clear-eyed and dignified, and very sure that his faith has given him strength and purpose to come, at last, to abiding peace.

21

Neil le Roux's Story

My ancestor was Gabriel le Roux, who arrived from Blois on the south bank of the Loire River in France. It was an area famous for its wheat, wine and chocolate. He was reputed to be a good winemaker and a good drinker. He arrived in Saldanha Bay on 13 April 1688. There have been Le Rouxs in the Valley from that date. My father was born in 1899, and his name was Daniel Marthinus. He was four years old when the farm La Provence was divided.

I was born on the original La Provence. My earliest memory is of going to church in Franschhoek. We were sixteen children and we walked in age order and filled the whole of the front row, which was our place in the church. Sunday was a day of quiet and reverence.

We got home and had a nice lunch. It was always at 12.30. All the children had to sit at the table, say their grace, and then eat a full cooked meal. Food was plentiful, and we had big appetites for the delicious piled plates. Supper was much simpler, usually soup, but what soup, with all the bones and vegetables. With good bread and farm butter, fruit was all we needed to be satisfied.

Every day for lunch, there was meat. We butchered all our own animals. We ate pork, chicken, lamb and beef. We had a big cool-room outside, which was made of mesh wire, with coal and wood-wool between the walls of mesh. It was constantly wet and became cold inside. The meat aged beautifully and was tender, with good flavour.

We made all our own butter, buttermilk of course, and cream cheese. I had the job of churning the butter. When it was all sepa-rated and washed, I had to pack it into the mould, and it would weigh a pound. The shop at La Motte would weigh it all again, and if it was a bit overweight they would send it back and say there was still water in it. So I was very careful. It was wrapped in greaseproof paper.

To bake our bread, my mother used five-gallon paraffin tins cut in half lengthways. We baked three times a week. We used seven of those baking tins. Three loaves a day fed the family. It was such a huge quantity of dough that my mother and some of the coloured women in the kitchen would all be kneading. I used to like doing it too.

We had a huge vegetable garden, and of course it was very pro-ductive because we had chicken, sheep and cow manure to put into the soil. We grew all our own vegetables, so we had potatoes, beans, spinach, pumpkins, rice, tomatoes, peas, onions and squash, sweet potatoes, carrots, parsnips, beetroot. The loft was full of sweet potatoes, potatoes, onions, pumpkins and squash, which were stored for winter.

We also stored loquats, which lasted very well. We had a quince hedge, and the huge quinces we picked while still hard. They ripened slowly, and were bottled or made into sambals and jam. There were guavas and crab-apples too, and it was nice to see all our food there.

Sundays were chicken days. We had huge chickens, Rhode Island Reds and Australorps, and we needed four or five to give everyone a nice helping. They tasted so different to what the chickens taste now. *Poeding* was mostly bread pudding, with lots of raisins, cinnamon and jam, or else stewed fruit, sago and baked custards. We ate a lot of fresh fruit, and grapes the whole season.

To play, we usually went up to Le Roux Village, which was another big piece of land owned by our family, across the main road. All of us were barefoot, and in season we would have *'n trossie druiwe in die sakkie*. We played all our favourite games, the coloured children played with us, and we were also at school together. We spoke mostly Afrikaans and some English.

One of the best games was *Jan Blou*. There were four in a team, and there were four large squares drawn into the ground. In each square there was one of your team, and the other team had to send one boy at a time to see if he could run through all four squares without being touched by the opposition. It was very energetic, and we were all screaming for our side. This game was strictly for boys – girls could only watch. We played cricket too, and then if it was a big match, the whole *dorp* came to see it.

We also played *bok-bok* and *klip-afgooi*. You put a big stone underneath, and then a smaller stone on top, then you had to stand four big steps back and with another stone knock the top stone off. It was quite difficult. We played *jukskei* and *blik-aspaai*, like hide-and-go-seek, with a big tin that you kick or smack to make a noise. We all had marbles, and stole the other best *ghoens* if we could.

When we got home we were very dirty from running around barefoot. There was a 'donkey' stove to heat bath water, and there wasn't enough water for everyone to bath every night, so we took turns. But we had to wash our feet and our faces and hands and teeth before we got into bed. The oldest brother had to check if we had washed them. A bit of rebellion was to wash only one foot, and when he came to check, you just put out the clean foot. My mother couldn't understand how the sheets were so dirty if our feet were clean, and so we were found out.

You could only get onto the school bus in the morning and the afternoon if you lived more than three miles away, and there was a big stone to mark the three-mile border. We were five hundred yards before the stone, so we would have to walk. The children who got off the bus just on the other side of the three-mile stone used to laugh at us having to walk home.

I finished matric at Franschhoek High School. My father said that two or three of the children must stay on the farm to continue it. No one else wanted to do that, so I stayed. I started to work for my father for two pounds a month and my board and lodging. I was working with the coloureds, pruning, cleaning vineyards, making the raisins from grapes, making wine, picking the peaches and plums. We had huge barrels and crushed all our own grapes, and only when the juice stopped fermenting did distillers come and pump it off into their tankers.

It was 1945, and because of the War not much of the wine was exported, so a lot of the farms dried some of the grapes for raisins. When they were dry, we sent them to Wellington Dried Fruit in Wellington to be packed. Raisins were packed with biscuits into the tins that Ouma Smuts sent to the South African troops wherever they were fighting during the War. Also in the tin was a pair of socks. All the women in South Africa were knitting socks for the troops up North.

We packed all of our own fruit for export. We had Santa Rosa, Gaviota, Kelsey and satsuma plums, and Kakamas and Early Dawn peaches. We made the flat *kissies* of wood that the fruit used to be packed into before cardboard and plastic. The pay for a hundred boxes was one shilling and sixpence, but I could make one with my eyes closed. Our label was 'La Provence, South Africa Calling' with the picture of a radio beacon sending out the message. All the fruit went to the United Kingdom.

You know how Middagkrans got its name, Gwen? My father told me. Lots of the people here didn't wear a watch, and especially not the workers. The farmers decided to paint a very big rock because they had noticed that at midday the shadow from the top of the mountain touched the rock. They painted it white, and every season they would go up to repaint the rock. They used to take a picnic and a few *doppies* and have a fine time. It was one of our rituals. It could be seen far down the Valley, and it gave everyone an idea of the time.

I must talk about the cattle. Every farmer in Franschhoek had cattle. None of them had big enough farms to graze the cattle, so during the summer the cattle from all the farms used to range along the mountains together. Each farmer had an identifying mark on his beasts, a clip on the ear or a brand mark.

I loved going up with my father and all the children, when we were young, to go and collect them for the trek to Langebaan. They had to go because there was not enough grazing for winter. It was during Easter school holidays, and a few of us used to take sheets of iron and make a rough house between two big rocks so that we were sheltered at night. First thing to do was to start a fire, to kill all the spiders, scorpions and snakes in between the rocks. When the fire was out, we used some grasses to sweep it all clean, and then we put out blankets and our food there.

Our food was beans, flour, salt and some oil. We had a big pot to cook in. We took *ketties* and shot guinea fowl, rock pigeons, partridges and pheasants, which are still to be found up on the mountain. We fished in the river, and everything we caught was cooked over a fire. We ate very well. When we wanted milk, we just milked the nearest cow.

I remember looking up at the heavens at the shooting stars, which I always thought I might catch, and the moonlight so bright you could still read a book at ten o'clock at night. And such a silence that covered the Valley, only the cattle moving nearby was what you heard. You saw the owls going about their business, and other raptors. It was a wonderful time – we had time to dream before progress arrived.

Some farmers rode out on horses, and began calling their cattle by name. The cattle used to range all the way to Villiersdorp, Wemmershoek and towards the Worcester mountains. But it was the strangest thing. Wherever they were, they turned as soon as the farmers called and began walking back to Franschhoek. By the second or third day, huge numbers could be seen miles away where they could not have heard the voices, but they somehow knew it was time to gather on the mountain. My uncle, who had the farm Beaucoup de Luc further down the Valley, would join us, and all the calves would walk beside their mothers. Once the cattle were all assembled and sorted, the farmer or the coloured herdsman would walk or ride a horse in the front, and the cattle would follow. Up to Paarl they would try to run back to the Valley, but once we got to the other side of Paarl there was not a moment's trouble – they just kept going until we got to Oudebosch, right along the lagoon at Langebaan.

As soon as the cattle were really on their way, farmers would go up on the mountain and start fires on a wide front. Sometimes the fires would last for three weeks. It was done to restore the pasture. They did it every year for as long as anyone could remember.

I was ten years old when I walked the whole distance with the cattle. Perhaps I took after my maternal Oupa – he was very strong. I had a wonderful time and felt very brave and important. We slept along the road, had a braaivleis at night, used to sing marching songs, rode on the cows, and we didn't bath at all. Some farmers still have their holiday houses there, on those grazing lands. It is part of the National Parks now, and called Oudebosch.

My mother's father, Oupa Piet Swanepoel, was a real toughie. He was ten years old when he was already breaking in the horses on the farm. A horse kicked him in the chest and he coughed blood for three weeks. His father believed that if you killed a cat, skinned it immediately and put the warm skin on the chest, it would stop the haemorrhage. Several cats gave up their skins, and the child did stop bleeding.

Mentioning cats reminds me of another story. A Polish medical photographer working in a laboratory with a cousin of mine reported on the doings of a cat in a laboratory in Warsaw, where she was thirty years ago. She had to photograph a human liver for research purposes. The liver had been removed at an autopsy and proved to be a medical rarity of great interest. She was setting up the lights and cameras, and she was called away for a minute. When she returned she saw the cat going through a window with the liver in its mouth. She screamed, and the resident pathologist rushed to her aid. They went chasing after the cat, which had to be sacrificed as it had already swallowed most of the liver. The photograph was a great success.

At fifteen Oupa Swanepoel joined the Boer commandos during the Boer War, which was the fight by the Dutch farmers against the might of Queen Victoria's armies. He was made a saboteur, and his speciality was blowing up railway lines. General de Wet understood that the boy had a breathing problem and issued him with a certificate so that all the army doctors, or sympathisers, should treat his chest free of charge, as he had no funds to pay for treatment. He was finally caught by the British and sent with other Boer prisoners to Ceylon. When the peace was signed in 1902, the officers in Ceylon asked all the prisoners to sign a paper declaring allegiance to King Edward of England, after which they would be put on a boat and sent home. Oupa Swanepoel flatly refused. He finally capitulated after six years, two of them spent as the last Boer in Ceylon.

Conditions were rough, but the worst for him was the unrelieved diet of rice and bananas. The prisoners used to make small boxes from food boxes they received, to trade with the guards or other prisoners for a little extra food. A bit of chicken or vegetables were dreamed about, to relieve the monotony of the rice. Escapes had been planned but never succeeded as the rules were strict. They also tried to sneak down to the harbour and get onto a boat, but that was futile as they were so clearly not from Ceylon.

When he got back to the Cape, he studied at Stellenbosch University. After he returned to his family home, he met a Miss Muller, got married and went to Klerksdorp, because the discovery of gold meant that business was good there. He had a butchery and bakery, and supplied bread to the mines.

He came back to Franschhoek after four years, as the business competition, mainly from the Jews, skilled in buying and selling, proved too much for him. He bought a shop in Franschhoek. Boland Bank built right next door to him, in the main road. A few years later, he opened another shop, in Le Rouxville.

Oupa Swanepoel wore a bag of garlic around his neck for the last forty years of his life, and died at 97. An autopsy showed that when the horse had kicked him, two ribs punctured his right lung, and it was, on his death, a small shrivelled organ the size of a tennis ball.

❖

Life continued, we all grew up. My older brothers got married, and I also started to look at girls. There were very few girls in the Valley because there was not work for them. The girls worked in Paarl, Wellington, Cape Town, Stellenbosch, even Calitzdorp. They took lodgings with a relative, or a family who had a spare room, or a boarding house.

You were not permitted to ask a girl directly to go out with you. You had to find a brother or a cousin to suggest it, and then give a couple of dates when it might be suitable. The go-between would then tell you which was the day she could come out, and where and what time you could fetch her. I bought a 1950 Morris, which I had fixed up, and that was a great advantage. I even had girl-friends in Calitzdorp; it took more than five hours to get there.

After any entertainment you had to take the girl home at exactly the right time, or her mother wouldn't let you into the house again. Occasionally there was a dance, which was very exciting. We wore tuxedos, and the girls wore long dresses and gloves. After you were engaged, you could buy a corsage and pin it onto your girlfriend's dress. So going out was very formal. When you said goodbye it was at the front door, and you left.

A date was going to the bioscope or to the drive-in. It couldn't be the drive-in on the first date – according to our mothers, that was very dangerous. Then afterwards, you went to a tearoom for a milkshake. Our entertainment in Franschhoek was in the Town Hall. Once a month someone came to show a film. It was Tarzan, cowboys and crooks, or sometimes a murder. The whole town came to watch.

I was 27 when I met Laura de Kok. She was teaching at the Franschhoek school. Laura was descended from Servaas de Kock, who came from Middelburg, Zeeland. He arrived from Holland in 1707 and married Suzanna van Booven.

Postscript

Laura had been teaching at the school in Hermanus. She taught all kinds of sport, and put on theatrical productions including operettas. To further her career, Laura left to go and live in Nieuwoudtville. Life was rather restricted there, so far away from civilisation, and so she applied for a post at Franschhoek High School, which she got. She was not there for long when she met Neil le Roux. She was boarding at the hostel for the teachers called Linquenda, which means 'I will have to leave one day'. It is now a guest house called La Fontein and has a steady stream of visitors.

Neil and Laura had a steady courtship – their values and interests were similar – and it was no surprise to both families when they declared their intention to get married.

22

Franschhoek Honeymoon

A friend of mine, whom I met in Johannesburg in the sixties, told me her story of a young couple.

The bride – let us call her Mary – was nineteen at the time. She and her husband had met each other at Cape Town University. They had a very proper courtship, and both families approved of the marriage. When he got his engineering degree they decided to marry almost immediately. She was radiantly in love. The wedding itself was a great success. Now the family fortunes had to be founded – after all, he was 22. His first job was on the construction of Wemmershoek Dam. They looked for a house to rent in Franschhoek, since it was close to his work.

They were shown several properties, but with a small budget

the choice was limited. The agent must have decided they were of solid and sober character and would be responsible. He took them to the Armstrong farm. The Armstrongs were older, with children all flown the nest, and they wanted to spend six months a year in England. They needed a reliable couple to live in the house during this time. The couple impressed them with their demeanour, enthusiasm and obvious affection for each other. Perhaps it reminded them of when they themselves were young. It was decided that the couple would move into the house within two weeks.

My friends moved in and found fortune was favouring them. The house was beautifully furnished. A lifetime of study had gone into assembling an exquisite collection of antiques. Paintings by noted artists covered the walls. Heavy silver cutlery was to be used each day. Branched silver candelabras stood on the fine dining-room table. Pure Irish linen sheets covered the beds, fine thread-work decorated the pillowslips on the antique mahogany four-poster bed in the main bedroom. Goose down filled the pillows, as it did the eiderdowns. A library of marvellous books on all topics showed the intelligence and enthusiasm of the collector. Living in such surroundings would be a life-shaping experience. All the bride and groom brought with them was their clothes. They had arrived in Paradise.

In this house of treasures, one stood above all the others. Her name was Emily – a beautiful matronly coloured woman who carried her body like a queen, with a bosom for small children to sleep on. She had an uncanny ability to sense her good purpose in life; and with her natural empathy, that purpose was to bring pleasure into the lives of those around her. Emily was also a wonderful and inventive cook. Mary had taken to having a mid-morning cup of tea with her each day. She learnt about Cape cooking by watching Emily prepare things for mealtimes, and heard the village gossip.

A week after the couple arrived, it was their first anniversary. They would have been married for a month. After her husband left for work, Mary was sitting companionably in the vast kitchen with

Emily, thinking how to make a memorable evening. She came from a family of celebrators. A special dinner there would be with all her husband's favourite dishes. But what would make this day or night really unforgettable? She confided in Emily. What could she do, out of the ordinary, to surprise her beautiful new husband?

'Merrim, I have got an idea. Come and look.' Emily led Mary into the back yard and out of a door into the garden. 'You see, this is what we will do. We will get the men after lunch to take the big bed from the bedroom and put it outside. Then when Little Master comes home, you don't let him go into the bedroom, but let him use the other bathroom. We can put on all the nice curtains for the bed, and when you are having supper, I will do something else out here.'

Mary was thrilled. The men were summoned, the bed assembled. Under Emily's supervision the perfect spot had been found. The house was L-shaped, and the inner corner was completely private from the road and passers-by. Here the bed was placed by a small willow, to look up towards the mountains. The canopy was in place, its delicate lace hangings moving gently in the breeze. It was February and hot, but the afternoon was cooling. It promised to be a balmy evening.

The supper that evening was a miracle. The couple sat down to a mushroom soup made with the wild mushrooms collected two hours before on the side of the mountain under the pine trees. The wild herbs, integral to the sauce, had been picked five minutes before. The crayfish ragout smelt of sea spray and waves crashing onto a beach. This ragout had been made first by Emily's great-grandmother, who lived at Langebaan. She passed the recipe down the female line in the family. It had a special combination of ingredients that was her secret, and it was magnificent. The malva pudding was also a much-treasured family recipe, poetic in its lightness, sinfully dark in its taste under thick cream. A special bottle of champagne, saved from their wedding, was opened.

They talked and laughed, feasted and held hands. They were so in love. But Mary had promised a surprise, and the young man insisted: What was it? Finally Mary relented. He was to prepare for bed, come out into the garden, and follow a trail of rose petals as it led him. The roses were in full bloom then, the obvious romantic touch.

But Emily had been busy too. Beside the rose petals she had put a long line of small candles nestled in paper bags filled with sand, and lit them. The trail of tiny lights made magic of the garden, and two magnificent candelabra stood at the end of the rose trail, one on each side of the bed. There was a further bottle of champagne chilling in a silver bucket on the night table, and two crystal glasses beside it. And there was Mary.

Many words of love were spoken, one to the other. We know what those words were: they are universal and enduring. It was a rapturous night. As dawn broke, they renewed their vows to one another and fell into a deep sleep.

Mary woke with the sun streaming into her eyes. There was a strange weight on her foot. She lifted her head. A cow was resting her neck on the footboard of the bed. Her muzzle lay on Mary's foot, and she started chewing the cud. Mary sat up, looked around, then rapidly sank down and pulled the sheets over her head. She tugged on her husband's arm so that he would not sit up.

The farm workers were sitting or standing around the bed in a wide circle. One very elderly man was sitting on a cool-drink box, cutting his toenails. The gardener was leaning on his rake, smoking a joint. An older woman with a face like a hen was perched on a stool, knitting a sock. Another woman in an advanced state of pregnancy was winding her hair into curlers. A married couple were having a wordless argument of many gestures so that they would not disturb the young lovers.

Someone had thoughtfully brought out mugs of early morning tea and rusks. Three shifty adolescent boys in school uniform were wondering out loud, 'Is hulle nou klaar?' A young woman, still in her pyjama pants but no top, was standing breast-feeding a naked baby, her copper shoulders catching the sun. The cow, swishing her tail to ward off the morning flies, continued her ruminations.

Emily, who had come from her own house, stopped in her tracks at what she saw. The folk scattered in all directions. 'They have got no manners, merrim, to look at you like that,' she said with feeling. 'They just wish it was like that for them.'

Nine months later to the day, the first of three sons was born to Mary and her husband, later followed by a daughter. They are all gifted, bright, beautiful and creative, and have children who are in that same mould. Perhaps the family recipe was used each time for their conception.

Curiously, the first farm I looked at in Franschhoek in 1985 was this one. The Armstrongs were long gone, but it was in the hands of equally charming people. I walked out to the delightful garden at the back of the house. The willow still stands, majestic now. I am sure that somewhere under the willow in the small garden I saw, there are still playful nymphs smiling in recollection of a heavenly evening, long years ago.

23

The Story of Mary and Peter May

Mary speaks

I was born in Franschhoek. My mother's name was Regina Floris. She had nine daughters, and I was the oldest one. She was never married and she never received any financial support from anyone, especially not her family. They were very unkind to her. They used to say, 'There goes that whore with her bunch of children.'

My Oupa and Ouma lived with us and looked after the small children. Then they found a little house on a farm, but when it was pension day they would still come home to Middagkrans and bring us a lot of groceries, as much as they could afford.

I was born in Paarl in 1948. My mother worked at the Jones factory. Jones was a canning factory for fruit and vegetables, mainly for export. When I was a few months old, my mother got work in Cape Town, so she took me to my Ouma for her to care for me.

When Mommy travelled to Franschhoek, she came on the steam train from Cape Town to Paarl. It was very slow and took almost all day. She changed trains at Paarl, and arrived in Franschhoek at one o'clock at night. We all had to get up, go to the station and meet her, and walk back to Middagkrans. It was about three kilometres. We got so tired.

She only came to visit at the end of the month. She brought home money for us, and sweets. Oh, I remember when Mommy came to visit – it was so wonderful! I used to cry and hang on to her because I had missed her so much. I got smacked when she left because I would not let her go, because I think it was just as hard for her to go away from us.

She used to bring little packets of peanuts which cost a tickey (three cents) a pound, so we got a lot of them; also beads made of coloured balls of sugar, which was like a necklace that you could eat. They were all different colours and flavours. Bananas, they were twelve for a shilling, therefore one penny each.

My mother then worked on Middagkrans farm in the vineyards. When I was very small, I was already picking up the *stokkies*. I also had to look after the small children.

I went to school when I was seven years old. It was the Congregational Church School in above the police station, between Academy Street and Dirkie Uys Street. I was clever. I was always in the first three in class position. My best subjects were History, Nature Study and Reading. I loved the concerts we had at the school or the church. We listened to music, sang and acted out stories. My mother had bought me the biggest plastic doll. I used to sing 'Doedoe, my Baba' and 'Baa Baa, Black Sheep', and the principal used to play the piano. The audience threw money onto the stage for all the children. Every class had to perform in some way. This was an annual event.

We went to Sunday school on the farm. One of Mr Smit's sons

gave us Sunday school. We were not in a hall – we sat on the lawn every Sunday. People were very God-fearing. In the morning was church for an hour, then just after lunch we went to Sunday school, and at five o'clock we went to town in the bakkie to attend the Congregational Church. Sundays were for church, God and showing respect. It was not a good day! We couldn't run or play or make a noise.

We went barefoot to church, with the biggest bows in our hair. Mommy made us all our own ribbons, which she made out of fabric. We were three girls by then. Christmas was the first time I wore a pair of shoes. I was eight years old, Katy was five, and Gina was two. We were all dressed the same with the full starched skirts, little bodices and puffed sleeves, and we had the taffeta lining skirts with an over sheer skirt printed with flowers. Then we all had our big ribbons in our hair.

We felt beautiful, with our white socks for the first time and the shoes. We used to play rugby on the lawn barefoot, and so my toes were always sore, and then, being unused to the shoes, my heels were always sore, but you didn't tell your mother because maybe she took them away. The first time I wore them I walked like a soldier, *clomp, clomp, clomp,* so that everyone could hear I had shoes. The soles were of thick leather, so they really made a noise. Now we were all ready for the Christmas party.

We used to buy crinkle paper. Mommy used to make all our decorations and for all the families on the farm, including the party hats. The crinkle paper she cut in long strips and then wound them in circles and glued them onto cardboard bases with starch. There were little strings to tie under the chin, and on the side were our huge bows sticking out underneath the hat.

Our farm party was held in the pack-shed, and we sat on fruit cases. Mrs Smit baked lots of cakes, and there were sweets and ginger beer. The families' sweeties were in a small piece of crinkle paper with your name on it. All the girls got a rag doll, and the boys got cars. All this was bought with the pennies which we had to hand in to the farmer right through the year on Sundays at our farm Sunday school.

The Christmas tree was a very big pine tree, all decorated. On Christmas Day in the morning there were three real silk stockings hanging on the end of our brass bed. Inside there were sweeties and peanuts, and then our own presents. It was always a rag doll. I had a lot of rag dolls.

We never danced on Christmas Day, we sang Christmas carols and other hymns – it was a holy day. There was no alcohol served, and it was only on New Year's Eve that there was alcohol and dancing. Everyone put on their Christmas caps for this party, and one could see the next morning who had been drunk, because the lower branches were full of caps that had been pulled off the tops of men's heads. New Year was always fruit-picking time, so *Tweede Nuwejaar* was a work day. It was only in the evening that there was still a bit of a party.

When I was nine years old, I was doing all the family washing. I first had to do all the white things, then I put them in the blue [starch] in a tin bath, and then they were thrown over the blackberry bushes to dry. All the tablecloths, all the aprons, and the Voortrekker *kappies*, all of them white, and the crocheted doilies, were put into starch. The *kappies* were worn all over the Valley by the women staff.

Then ironing day was on Tuesday. I took the starched washing, then sprinkled it with water and rolled everything loosely, and started ironing when I came home from school. It was with a flat-iron, and we had four of them, so while I was using one, then the others were getting hot. There was a *lappie* to keep them clean, and you had to test the heat with a bit of spit on the finger, to know when to use it.

You had to do this very neatly, there must not be one wrinkle or crease on any piece of the laundry, otherwise Mommy would get cross. I was taught to fold all the linen as smooth as the pages of a book. I used to stand and look at it with great pride. All the shirts for school looked as if they had just come from a shop, they were so nicely folded. Mommy always checked my work. I learned very well.

When Peter [Mary's husband] used to come home with holes in his *broeks*, I knew exactly how to make the best patches. All my cupboards were so tidy, because I was taught so well by my mother.

When I was nine or ten, during the holidays, and in June when it snowed, I was working in the orchards and also in the vineyards. We used to work after school, there were never times to play – life was always working. For all of this I got a half a crown a week, or two and sixpence.

December was time to pick fruit, and then the fruit cases were made of wood, and we had to arrange the wood-wool in the cases for the other packers to fill. The first peaches were the Early Dawns, then the Culemborg, then the Van Riebeeck, and then the Rhodes. These were all export peaches. Boland peaches were not for export as they bruised too easily, so they went to the Cape Town market in Sir Lowry Road.

When I was eleven years old, I was finished with school, in Standard 5. There was a tradition that when you left school, you picked up the front of your school dress and it was filled with raisins made from hanepoot grapes, and also peanuts. Those raisins were so fat and juicy and sweet, you couldn't get enough. They make them much too dry these days, but then it was the most special treat. They were made in Wellington, and a lot of the second-class grapes from the Valley used to go there.

You had to be careful how high you lifted your skirt because your bloomers, which were made of navy interlock fabric and came down your legs in *pypies*, would stick out. Then everyone would laugh. But if you lifted your skirt higher, then you got more sweets and raisins in it, and you could take more home for the younger children.

When I was twelve years old, I went to work in Cape Town for some Indian people. They were Moslems. The women wore a sari, and the men wore long white trousers and a long white over-shirt. On their heads the men wore a *keffiya*, and the women wore long winding scarfs around their head and neck. They were very fastidious people and very clean. There were basins of water, and cloths for washing your hands and face whenever you had touched food or gone to the bathroom, or if you came in from outside.

They wore beautiful clothes, in wonderfully rich fabrics. They were made of silks and brocades and thin fine cottons. These things all came from the East. Long shawls were edged with gold embroidery of a rich and elaborate pattern.

I did work in the kitchen and the house. For breakfast they ate fruit and toast. The main meal was in the evening, and then it was a feast. The men were all running shops and trading during the day. When the supper was all ready to be served, everyone sat round the table, the large extended family, old and young. The main dishes were curries, and they were very strong and hot. There was always a lot of water on the table to drink, to cool the fires. There were rotis, *dhaltjies*, samoosas, fresh every day. Vegetables were mixed, first sliced and then cooked. All of it was bought daily. There was a lot of butter added, and everything was delicious.

They brought their own masala from India, and they used to crush it on a stone and then put it into a mortar. They had their own ginger and garlic growing in the garden, which were added to the coconut and coconut milk. They had an amazing stone. It was flat, but with a long hollow down the centre and another stone fitted into the hollow. Everything in the hollow was pounded with the stone that fitted in the top. It was amalgamated in the most perfect way.

What made the curries so wonderful was the ginger, garlic, grated coconut and butter, and also the masala. This was fried with the meat, chicken or lamb. They taught me to make very good curries and biryanis. They really taught me very well, I have never forgotten the recipes. They also taught me to make doughnuts, koeksisters, and the most delicious cakes, scones, crunchies and tarts.

Those Indian people were very good to me, and just like my family. Their name was Shabodien. I was with them for five years, and they were remarkable people for their kindness and concern. Their good manners taught me a lot that I thank them for.

Then I went back to Franschhoek when I was seventeen years old. Opposite where Susan Huxter lives, there was the Kamrick Hall. We had movies, and we had dancing on a Saturday night. Someone had to open the door and switch on the lights for the people coming in, and I saw this man. Right away he asked me my name, and from the beginning 'he was making eyes at me'. His name was Peter May. After a little while he became my boyfriend.

❖

Peter

Peter was born in Salt River in 1937. His father was a hawker, with a little handcart. He sold fruit and vegetables all over the district, and also went into District Six for some of his customers. He also had a little vegetable stall on the side of their road, and all the housewives used to come to him for their fresh vegetables. His mother was a drunk and didn't look after him at all or any of the other children. His uncle and auntie lived with them, and Auntie used to look after him as his mother was always drunk and didn't want to work either. His father died when he was three years old.

He was sent to attend the Eureka Catholic School in Elsies River, and left when he was sixteen years old. He had passed Standard 6. He got his first job, which was in a ceramics factory. He used to shape the clays over the moulds to make plates and bowls, then pack them all into the furnace. He earned five pounds a month.

He then went to work in an ice factory that was in Woodstock, on the hill overlooking the harbour of Cape Town. All the ice was loaded onto trucks and then driven down to the docks and loaded into the holds of the deep-sea trawlers. When the fish came up in the nets, they were put directly on top of the ice.

He was working for I&J. One of his duties was to clean out the waste pipes of the ships. These huge pipes were filled with all the stomachs, fins and offal of the fish. It was all pumped into the harbour at the time. One day, standing on North Quay where the aquarium is today, he fell off the ship and got sucked under the boat towards the propeller. He stripped off his heavy waterproof jacket and pants, got out of his underwear, and managed to kick his way up to the side of the boat. He was pulled up naked but alive.

He was a bodybuilder, and had lots of girlfriends. He remembers driving around in a Cadillac 'just like Elvis used to have'. His brother-in-law came to fetch him one Saturday afternoon because he was taking a drive upcountry and had heard that the Franschhoek girls were pretty and warm and good dancers. Peter arrived at the Kamrick Hall and was soon helping put up the microphone for the band, and was then asked to be the doorman for a while.

He opened the door, and there stood a girl dressed in red. Her name was Mary. She loved red, and had a red cloak when she was younger, and was called Red Riding Hood. He was smitten – it was love at first sight for him, and later for Mary too. He drove up every Saturday evening to be with her, and found the separation during the week so unbearable that he left his job and found work in Franschhoek.

He was, for the first time in his life, absolutely madly in love. He was eleven years older than Mary and didn't want her to have another boyfriend. There was very little work around at the time aside from odd jobs, and after some months they decided to go together to Cape Town.

❖

Mary speaks

We found jobs in Fish Hoek together, Miss Gwen, and at last were at the sea. I worked in a hotel, cleaning rooms, and in the kitchen. We met such a lot of very nice people. My boyfriend, Peter, worked as a barman. We were there for two years, but then we came back to Franschhoek.

So then we moved on to a farm owned by Danny Brewster. We had two rooms and a kitchen. We bred our own chickens, on the back of the wagon in a big mesh-wire box – so we had our own eggs, and we ate the chickens when they got older. Then we had the chickens in one room, and we slept in the other room. I had bricks and a piece of flatiron, and we made a fire underneath and did all the cooking on that.

My first child, Brian, was a few months old when my mother came to ask if she could stay with us. She didn't want to stay alone on the old farm as there were too many problems there. I told her she had to ask Peter because it was his house, so she asked him and he said she could stay with us at any time. There was a spare room, so she moved in with some of her children, and also brought some of her furniture with her. We all got on very well, she was the most wonderful person I have ever met. Then my second child was born on this farm.

When we were small, my mother made us such beautiful dresses. Underneath the top shirt, the petticoat material had flowers on it. The dresses had a shiny lining and layers of fabric over the top. She got the material in Franschhoek, on the corner where Spar is now. It was a very big shop, and at one end there were rolls and rolls of material, more than you can imagine. Sometimes there was even material from overseas, but that we couldn't afford.

We had an Auntie who came to visit regularly. She worked in the textile mills in Salt River, where coloured families had worked for two or three generations, and she could tell us the history of most of the material in that shop – where the rough cottons came from, how they were processed, and about the shine of the evening fabrics for dance dresses which lit up the back of the shop. The material was so cheap, and many women made their children's clothes.

There isn't one coloured person who was not taught ballroom dancing when they were small. So everyone had two or three dance dresses. It was really our only social life, and with the musicians.

We also had matching ribbons, made out of fabric, for our hair. They were really big ribbons, and we thought we were so smart.

My husband got about five rands per week. It was with Danny Brewster. In the summer we worked on the fruit and the vines, in winter he grew vegetables like potatoes and sweet potatoes and cabbages. Then Mr Brewster moved to the town. Another man bought the farm, and then there was great hardship. My husband took a short holiday, he was exhausted. There were no holidays allowed! We worked the whole year, but there were no holidays. The farmer said he didn't like it that Peter took a week off (in three years); the other *volk* would start thinking they could also have a holiday. We decided to go.

The day we moved, it never stopped raining. Oh, it rained, everything got so so wet! But when the last load went on the tractor, my mother said they must come back because she was also coming with us. The farmer had said she could stay, because she was such a good packer. She packed all the fruit for export, and she was a very good worker. But she said, No, if we were going she was also going.

We arrived at the Collins's farm, we got a place there. They arrived on the farm in February and we arrived in March 1974. They came from Botswana and he could not speak Afrikaans. Fortunately, my husband could speak a little English and so they could understand each other.

We moved into a one-bedroom house. We had to pack things around us and on top of us, in the rafters of the roof. After a short time Mr Jack decided we could not live like that, and we moved into a three-bedroom house where my mother had her own bedroom and I had my own bedroom.

Sometime later, I heard from other women in the village that the municipality had set aside more land in Groendal to build coloured housing. We had to go to the municipal offices, show our identification book, take some pay slips, and sign some documents. I did not say a word to Peter, but the idea of owning my own home was like a dream to me. You would get the plot and all the building materials, but the building was for us to do at our own cost.

Years went by and we heard nothing. We thought it was one of those things that governments tell you, and it never comes true. But eight years later, someone came to see me at work and told me I must come immediately to choose my piece of ground. I slipped out alone and went to have a look. I decided that a corner plot would be the most valuable, and also you would only have neighbours behind the house. That was the one I chose, and when I went home I had to tell Peter.

He was so amazed, we walked in the dark to go and see it because he didn't believe me, even the children came with us, and we fell on our knees right there to thank the Lord that we would, for the very first time in our lives, have a permanent home.

Our building material was delivered some months later. We had to build a little shack for Peter to sleep in, otherwise all the material would have been stolen. When we had built three rooms, we moved in, and then built slowly as we could afford it.

It's funny, Miss Gwen, but I want to tell you, we were in the house for about two years and were fast asleep at night. Peter woke with an angel tapping his arm. I woke up and I saw the light shining around him. The angel told him to be very quiet and just look up, which I did, and there was a huge black man in the bedroom with a long knife, leaning over Peter. Peter just said, 'Mary, give me my gun,' and the man ran out of the house. He had already collected all our food and blankets and clothing to take away.

We went to wake other people to find him. There was a tiny light on in another house. There he was sitting in the kitchen eating a tub of ice-cream while the owners slept. We made a terrible noise and caught him, and tied him up until morning when the police took him away.

❖

When Mary's beloved mother died, it was found she had been paying three funeral policies. There was a lot of money there to pay for a funeral, and more left over. Mary discussed with two of her sisters how they should spend the money. They decided they wanted to honour the mother who had borne such hardship for all of them and had never been anything but the most loving and dedicated mother. She had loved flowers, and Mary ordered the very best flowers from all the florists. There were lilies, carnations and delphiniums – and roses and roses. Mary ordered the best coffin and the most luxurious hearse to drive to the graveyard.

They had decided to have the eulogy in the church. At the last minute it was agreed that Mary, being the eldest, should make a reading. She wanted to speak from the heart and tell her truth. Her wealthy uncles were sitting in conspicuous opulence with their families. Mary stared at them and spoke of the pain her mother had endured, being an unmarried mother; the vilification by that part of the family; the unopened doors when she was in need; the rejection she had suffered from that branch of the family.

She spoke, for herself and her eight sisters, of the great love they had borne their mother, the enduring courage she had displayed in feeding all of them, and giving them real values and as much education as she could.

There was extended applause except from the uncles, who left hurriedly with their families. 'Miss Gwen, I never regretted it. My mother's grave and all the surrounding ones were deep in flowers. I knew she had seen it all and that she understood why I did it.'

I asked Mary, who is a serene and gracious woman, what her thoughts were on living through hardship and still having a happy marriage and fulfilled family life.

'Miss Gwen, your life is like a book,' she said calmly. 'I believe you must always be courteous to everyone, especially your family. I don't think you should stress other people, and don't make your problems theirs, or their problems yours, unless they are children. I put all of the problems on the table, and then we can't leave until we have a solution and we are all in agreement. That has always worked for me and Peter. We had our hard times but our love has never been in doubt, and our children had the right values to choose good men.'

This story might not seem so full of courage to people without knowledge of the political structures of the day. It is worth reminding other women that there is always hope to be had and progress to be made if you have belief in yourself. Mary had been given that inestimable gift by her mother.

24

Mammie's Last Goodbye

For the farm labourers there were no such things as holidays away. There was little spare cash, and responsibilities at home. The men had two weeks off at Easter, but the women seemed to go on and on, largely to keep an eye on the men, I think.

Seeing that a change is as good as a holiday, the women swapped jobs for a week or two on another farm; so the neighbour's maid might well arrive at my door on the Tuesday after the Easter week-end, or it could be someone quite unknown who had been sent to me. Before this all took place, there was much exchanging of information on merrim's temperament, the food, tea breaks, whether children were permitted to come along, and how hard the work was.

On this morning I was expecting Alice, a middle-aged woman

who sometimes picked fruit for me. I heard knocking, opened the door, and there stood Betty. Betty was four foot ten inches tall, a pale parchment yellow, of Bushman ancestry and very weathered. When she smiled, the puckering in her face came together as if one had pulled a thread, gathering in all the lines. She made up for shortness by having opinions. She made up for her lack of education by having opinions about everything.

'Môre, merrim, ek is hier,' she announced.

'Yes, but Betty, I am expecting Alice.'

'No, merrim, she comes not, her mother last night died. But she comes to tell you all, she told me I must come here, and she will come later.' Oh, I think, a storytelling requires certain props. In the case of death and sadness I had made a list. It was: brandy, tissues, brandy, aspirins, brandy, coffee and biscuit, brandy and lots of time.

'Ja dan, Betty, kom binne, wat weet jy van huisskoonmaak?'

'Oh, not nothing, merrim, maar gee my koffie, ek is dors.' She came into the kitchen and peered down corridors. 'Merrim, jy moet my nie los nie, ek sal verdwyn, die huis is so groot.'

Coffee drunk, I suggested we start cleaning the bathrooms. I went down the corridor, then through the bedroom and into the first bathroom. Betty was not behind me. I returned to the bedroom and found her standing next to our bed holding up a photograph of me. She turned to look at me and then looked at the photograph again.

'What are you doing?' I asked.

'Ek kyk net. Maar jirre, jy was baie mooi, Miz Gwen.'

Something in her voice and the past tense irritated me. 'What do you mean, I *was* pretty, Betty?'

She looked at me, then said matter-of-factly, 'Nee, merrim, nou is jy finish en klaar.' We went into the bathroom together.

We were making mild progress when there was knocking on the door, and it was indeed Alice. She inspected the preparations on the table. 'Oooo, merrim is so good, I now am telling you everything from the beginning.'

'Yes, Alice,' I said, 'tell me what happened to your mother.'

'Well, you see, merrim, dit was Mammie se verjaarsdag. En my groot broer, he come to celebrate with us, die een wat *daar* bly, by Moorreesburg, en Mammie sou sewe-en-sestig gewees op die dag, en ons wou 'n party maak.'

We paused. Country stories are always interspersed with back-tracking, interjection, eating and drinking. Sometimes they get seriously confused. Brandy was sloshed into a glass and a biscuit sucked on, coffee drunk, nose blown, aspirin swallowed.

'En my broer van Kaapstad, die een met die groot geel Buick, and also my susters from Wellington, and also the one from Simon's Town. I was wanting really to cook good like you, Miz Gwen, so I ask my brother to bring half a sheep.' She drew breath and had another long swallow of KWV five-year-old liqueur brandy. 'My broer het 'n skaap gebring, and can you believe, Miz Gwen, that just on that Saterdag midday you know, the kok Master Paul had ...'

There was a long pause, she lost her train of thought, a tear trickled down her face. Hoping to be helpful, I found myself asking Alice about Paul's cock.

'Yes, merrim, net so het hy net oorgeval en gevrek. Merrim, die kok and two hens het gevrek, net by die kombuisdeur. I tried to get him up, but he was stone dead. I tried, merrim, I tried, but that kok, jislaaik, he was dead. And also the two hens, dead.' She sloshed another brandy into her glass and tipped it down.

'Well, merrim, dit was so gelukkig, net op die dag van die party right there in front of me. And I just thought, Our Dominee he said, God works in mystery ways, if God did want us to eat chicken for Mammie's birthday, I am not to worry.'

I speculated on how the fowls had met their end.

'Ag, Miz Gwen, die kossies was so heerlik, the sheep on the braai was too wonderful, and the kok and those hens, Miz Gwen, met soet patat en boontjies, and a very big pampoen we found left in the fields, ja, dit was net wonderlik! And then with the ice-cream, the bargain pack from the shop, it is good. En dan het ons gesing en gedans, en 'n bietjie wyn gedrink. En toe sing ons al die outydse liedjies, en al weer gedans, en just when I was going to give out all the poeding, Mammie start to feel funny, and she said, "Alice, give me my pudding now, give me a spoon quickly, I'm feeling funny," and she just put it in her mouth, dan val sy dwars op die vloer, just like you threw a bag of potatoes, and she look at me and say, "My kind, ek is Goodbye," en toe is sy mos dood, really dead.'

Alice collapsed sobbing onto the table. It took time, but there was more to come.

'Ja, nou, my broer he run to the Dokter, and it was lucky he just come home from a party and he came, and he said, "Ja, Mammie is dood," and he make out the paper.' She sniffed, and wiped her face. 'Now this morning, ek was by die polisiestasie. Jy sien, Miz Gwen, as jou ma nou vrek, you must tell the police it was not foul play.'

'Oh yes,' I agreed, 'and then what?'

'Then I was by Baas Sannie.' Sannie is the municipal officer and general fixer and finder in the village. His portfolio includes allocating burial plots. 'He give us a plot, merrim, en dit het 'n lekker uitsig. Mammie can enjoy the view, she always said that when she sat on our stoep she could see all the vines and …' Her voice trailed away. Another tear slid down her cheek. Her wet hand slipped a bit on the bottle as she poured again. She sniffed loud and long. 'Then I went to Mr Pepler,' she said.

Something happens when one keeps company with people to whom nothing is strange. I know that Mr Pepler and his brother are the most excellent butchers, amiable and obliging, and the purveyors of the best mutton in the Boland. I try to see a link between the butcher and the coming funeral – but Alice is ready to go on.

'Jy weet ons het nie geld nie, en ons kan nie 'n mooi kis koop.' She sobbed again. 'You see, Mammie used to clean the floors twice a week, en jy weet die boere, hulle sit hulle moddervoete dwarsoor alles, dan Mammie, she cleaned that floor so you could see your face is shining so much in it. Mr Pepler, the one with the belly, not the other one, he said he could do me a big favour. You see we can't also afford a hearse, so nice Mr Pepler, he said he would take the coffin in the meat van, then he would save the money for us. En jy sien, he is used to riding around with dead meat in his bakkie, maar as die deure nie toe sal gaan, kan hy nie dit doen, want die customers wouldn't like to see a coffin, even if Mammie is also dead meat.' I found her some more tissues and poured the coffee.

'So,' she continued, 'I also went to the Posmeester.' She was limp from crying and put the coffee mug shakily back onto the table. 'You see, Mammie also polished the floors at the post office, and you know about the farmers and their muddy boots.'

'Yes, Alice, we have spoken of it already,' I said. I stroked her hand, trying to see the connection between the post office's floors and taking a coffin to the burial ground.

'Yes, but they walk from the butcher to the post office. So the Posmeester, hy sê hy kan my help. If the doors of the Peplers' van do not close over the coffin, then he will give Bertie, the technician, his lunch hour at three o'clock, and he can drive the coffin because their van is much longer than the other one, and the coffin will fit in. Dan gee ons Bertie 'n mooi bottel wyn.'

Alice was suddenly drained. I realised that three hours had passed. 'Well, Miz Gwen,' she said, 'die kinders sal nou by die huis wees, and I must walk home.'

Betty appeared out of nowhere. 'I am finished also, merrim, and I go walk home with Alice,' she said.

Alice got to her feet and gave a great sigh. 'Ek … uuuh, ummm … dink dat as Miz Gwen nie omgee nie, jy weet die aande is nie lekker nie sonder Mammie.' She sucked on her teeth. Two more of the brandies went home with her.

When Alice came to work two days later, it was reported that the funeral was a great success. Alice said, 'I was so sorry that Mammie was not there, sy sou dit so-o-o geniet het. She would have liked to have such a nice party after missing her birthday.'

25

The Dinner Party

Winter and early spring are good entertaining months in Franschhoek. The weather induces one to indulge, and friends who don't communicate during the picking season are able to do some conversational catching up.

I decided to include an attractive couple, new in the village, to join us. One of our guests, a wine merchant, had been talking to me about giving cooking lessons to a group of men. They needed to know more about the subject, particularly how to marry wines to food with more finesse. He decided he would come up to the house before his wife and spend two hours in the kitchen cooking with me.

Since it was snowing on the mountains I decided that the menu would be:

Vegetable and chicken-liver terrine with wine jelly and
spring onions
Olive-oil bread
Seven-hour roast lamb, whole onions, white beans and
parsnips, roasted garlic and olives
Mixed salad
Gorgonzola, Brie, Camembert
Almond soufflé with tangerine sauce (hot)
Fallen chocolate soufflé (warm)
Coffee

Tim arrived looking supremely nonchalant. He is big-boned,
attractive, with dark hair; open-faced and very clever. I took him
into the kitchen to get on with the cooking. I offered him an
apron. 'What for? I'm not going to get dirty,' he said. Fine with me,
I thought.

Since the lamb had already been in the oven for four hours
there was nothing to do on that score. We cut spring onions,
peeled parsnips, rinsed the beans, and unmoulded the chicken terrine, all the while continuing with a relaxed conversation. 'Cooking is not difficult,' he remarked. 'I could do this easily.' I reminded
him that, so far, we had not even turned on the stove, and he had
not yet cooked anything.

I thought we could get the *panade* ready for the soufflés, and
started to explain just what was involved. He elected to melt the
chocolate in a double boiler, and to grind the fresh almonds for the
hot soufflé. His attention was diverted by the unaccustomed activities, and the double boiler spat water all over the glass-topped
stove, popping and hissing as it went.

'What the hell is happening, Gwen? I just turned my back on
that damn thing for a minute,' he said.

'Just stay calm, we have a long way to go,' I assured him.

He flicked the switch to grind the almonds without putting the
lid onto the liquidiser. The almonds flew out vertically and settled
on the counter and the floor. He stood with hands on hips. There

were chocolate smears on his trousers and shirt. 'Can't I do something easier?' he asked. 'I think I should be wearing a crash helmet.'

In my kitchen, whoever makes a mess has to clean it up. I handed him a dry cloth to pick up the almonds. He watched me stir the flour into the butter, and then add the milk. We made a bit of progress. He managed to open the oven and add vegetables to the casserole without injury to himself, but spilt oil on his shirt. I then explained about beating the egg whites, adding them to the *panade*, and the correct cooking time for the soufflé. It should arrive puffed and golden at the appropriate time, twenty minutes after we had all finished the main course.

'I'm sorry,' he said, wiping a hand across his forehead, 'I am not getting involved in any more of this. I have never heard of anything with more potential for a monumental fuck-up than a soufflé. I am going to relax in the library with Bill and drink.'

The guests trickled in an hour later. It was cold outside, but there was a roaring fire in the library and lots of red wine to drink. Last of all came the unknown couple. He was dressed in a sturdy anorak, with thick pullover and corduroys. She was covered from head to foot in black. A large black hat covered most of her face. We could see dark eyes and very pale skin. A high-collared coat fell from her nose to the floor. Black boots with stiletto heels and black gloves completed the ensemble. She was inarticulate during the introductions. She is shy, we thought.

I suggested we go to the dining-room, as supper was ready. She stood up and took off her coat. A skin-tight dress clung to her shapely figure like Gladwrap. The problem was where the dress ended. When my sister and I were very young and had just started bathing by ourselves, my mother would say to us, 'Wash up as far as possible, then down as far as possible. Then wash possible.' 'Possible' was at the specific latitude of the hem of this woman's dress. It left every inch of quite incredibly gorgeous legs visible. The assembled men fell silent, as one might in the presence of true beauty. The men wanted to feast their eyes on those legs, but instead they shuffled about and didn't dare look at their wives. She had kept on her gloves and hat.

I had seated her between the aspiring cook and a bachelor botanist. She sat down. I hastily put a large linen table napkin on her lap. In a seated position, the tiny dress had slid further upwards. One could almost read the label on her pantyhose. I didn't want a murder done at the table.

The first course was served. There was much village chit-chat, to which she contributed nothing. She was cocooned in some dream state. Her husband seemed an amiable fellow and fitted in very well. I noticed she had not touched the food.

We were settling into the main course when she took off her hat, tossing it over the back of her chair. She had a lot of long dark hair piled into a chignon, which she now proceeded, like Rapunzel, to let down. It fell almost to her waist, a shining cascade of beautiful mahogany silk. She groped in her large handbag, which was hanging over the arm of her chair. She brought out a long black comb and inspected it. Taking a thick hank of her hair in her hands, she combed it from crown to tip over Tim's dinner. She kept her gloves on all the while.

Sensibly, Tim moved his plate further to the left, away from her. He also nudged his chair a few inches to the left. I was sitting next to her husband, at the other end of the table. He kept glancing nervously in her direction. Being the hostess, I chatted on, hoping to divert the others from her curious behaviour. She had continued combing all the while, gracefully going through a private ritual of grooming more appropriate to a bathroom. Her wide pale mouth held a secret smile. I asked her if she would like to make use of the facilities. She wouldn't, no, she was quite comfortable where she was. The combing continued.

Everyone on both sides of the table had now shuffled up towards me so that the same fate should not befall their dinner. She and my partner, at the far end of the table, were sitting in splendid isolation. They looked like the opposing team at a disarmament conference. My partner was manfully speaking of his favourite operas, those containing incidents of eccentrically behaved women. Perhaps he hoped she should feel supported. I doubt she had noticed anything unusual about what she was doing. She smiled at him and went on combing her tresses, now in his direction. He was obliged to shift his plate to the right.

I went to the kitchen to see about the soufflé. In the kitchen I could give way to laughter and listen to the others, who were busily concocting stories to hide their mirth at the weird conduct of our new guest. The maid, Dinie, was mystified. 'Merrim, wat maak daai vrou met haar hare, and why are you all sitting so far away from Master?' It was really hard to explain. I served the soufflés, to acclaim, and passed the Edelkeur. I noticed she had shed her gloves.

Finally I suggested returning to the library, where we could snuggle round the fire. At long last her husband decided that action was called for: he indicated she should sit on the carpet at his feet. He was sitting on the sofa. He opened his legs and locked her between them. Her arms were over his knees and she was unable to move. The next hour passed without incident.

At a gap in the conversation, he stood up and helped her to her feet. They could really not stay any longer; they did have small children and the hour was late. She started to get dressed. Her husband fetched her hat from the dining-room floor, and helped her with the gloves. Her hair was now securely pinned under the hat. The men took a last yearning look at the wonderful legs before Bill helped her with her coat. She turned to me and addressed me for the first time that evening. 'Gwen, it was wonderful, we will come again.' She grabbed me by my shoulders and kissed me very firmly in my left eye.

Once they were safely down the drive, we could give in to our merriment. 'What do you think she had drunk? Or was she on some medication she couldn't handle?' Everyone had an opinion. The men were sad their wives wouldn't be inviting the couple to dinner. Her husband was most jolly and decent and, by God, she had the most amazing legs.

I think Franschhoek or its inhabitants did not suit them. Only a few months later, they left for greener pastures. As for Tim's career as a chef, I don't think it took off; but his wife is most accomplished and their invitations to dinner are much sought after!

26

The Russian Invasion

I had been out shopping in Paarl for a dinner that Friday evening. I also had guests for Sunday lunch. Dinie had a message for me. 'Mr John said you must phone him.' I called John.

'Um, uh, Gwen, how are you? Could I ask you something?'

'Yes, of course,' I said, 'what do you want to ask?'

'Do you know anything about Russian food?'

'Very little, but a bit. I have cooked a few Russian meals to serve after the ballet and things like that.' I am curious. It's Franschhoek in midsummer, what are we expecting?

He continued. 'Well, umm, I was just wondering if you would be able to cook a Russian meal for me.'

John is one of my favourite people. 'Of course I can. But not this weekend, I'm busy. Anyway you are coming for lunch on Sunday. We can discuss it then.'

'Well, not really, Gwen, because it's for tomorrow. A small group of Russians are coming over, and there will be about twenty-four people.'

Oh really, thinks I, a piece of cake! Why did I ever learn to cook? A small group of Russians have just jetted over to have a Russian meal in Franschhoek. Improbable, it sounded to me.

There was a great deal of muttering and groaning, but in the end, as he knew, I said I would do it under certain conditions. The conditions were that he did all the shopping after I had composed the menu; and then delivered the ingredients to my kitchen, and sent someone up in the late morning to fetch me and all the food. Right, a deal was done. The only thing now was to get a menu and ingredients faxed down to John and send him off to do all the shopping.

All went according to plan, and John and his housekeeper, Pinkie, arrived later with mountains of ingredients for me to turn into the Russian feast. I heard a little more of the impending guests. De Beers had brought over some senior geologists from Siberia to take a look around South Africa – part work and part tourism – and they were coming up from Cape Town the following morning. A day in the country: how very Chekovian!

John owned one of the more beautiful historical estates in the Boland, and this was to be the venue. He had visited Russia many times during his career and thought it appropriate to reciprocate. His hospitality was renowned, and his generosity, originality and thoughtfulness made him an unforgettable host. I cooked for him on a regular basis, so I couldn't let him down.

My own dinner was organised and almost done. I started sorting out the priorities for the Russians. Their menu was to be composed of:

> Chilled borscht with dribbles of sour cream and *piroshki*
> Salmon *coulibiac* with Russian salad

Grape *kissel*

Kasha

Fresh raspberries and blueberries

I woke up at six the next morning and got stuck into all the preparation. By eleven things were almost under control. Right: shower, get dressed, put on my make-up, and then go down to John to put it all in place. Norman came to fetch me at the appointed time.

The first thing I noticed, fluttering from the flagpoles down the drive, was Russian flags. Communist-type flags! Blazing the Hammer and Sickle, the Afrikaner nationalists' worst nightmare, and right here in the Boland! This was vintage John. Two large men prowled the courtyard singing soulful songs, each with a balalaika across his chest. I caught the words 'Siberia' and 'Volga'.

The bar was set up. It was covered in icy stalactites of vodka, vast numbers of them. They looked like a mini-Ice Age. It was the Franschhoek formula at work: multiply the number of people by five (bottles, that is). But vodka was stronger than wine. Ah, I had not yet met the Russians.

Tables had been set up under the pergola. All was ready. I got my staff into the kitchen with me and we did what chores were still necessary. People were arriving all the time. In fact, the convoy of Russians and seven nubile girls arrived at the same time. The girls had been rounded up to provide extra female company because the Russians had been quite taken with South African women. These particular Russians were educated and well travelled. Some of them had lectured at American universities. They spoke heavily accented English.

John came out to greet everyone. He was wearing a military jacket of tremendous age, probably dating from the First World War. His entire chest was decorated with medals commemorating feats of daring down four generations. He came from a line of men who had served their country in times of crisis. He himself had served in the Black Watch, and had been wounded in Palestine as a young man during the Second World War.

On his head was a bearskin hat, and an elderly pistol lay in the belt of his trousers. The Russians blinked for a moment, hardly expecting someone who looked like a refugee from time past to come out of the house. Recognising him, they greeted him enthusiastically. They were all friends of long standing.

I introduced myself and asked the tour leader what the group had seen of interest and where he had taken them. The answer was 'Everywhere!' – Simon's Town, Cape Point, Clifton Beach, Kirstenbosch, up Table Mountain, the Waterfront, Cape Agulhas, a Pick 'n Pay hypermarket, where they had wanted to be photographed with a leg of lamb in each hand. Oh, the food you have, the abundance, and the wine and the women. They didn't want to leave, ever.

'The vomans are so beautiful and thin. They have the faces of angels. Their bosoms are absolutely perfections! They dress in such clothing, to allow one to look and touch.' Well, yes, there is a difference in women's choice of garments if the temperature is 30 degrees below freezing, or 30 above, as it was on this particular day. The female company were like a smorgasbord for connoisseurs of beauty, which they were.

Their vocal appreciation was soaked up by all us women, used as most of us were to the typical local male response to our efforts to look gorgeous, which could be along the lines of 'Did you do you hair?' or, what I had endured some years previously, 'Are you going to go out looking like that?' – said with a pained expression.

Vodka was poured into iced glasses. Even in minuscule ones I knew my limitations. Conversations were getting louder, great bursts of laughter erupted, everyone was enjoying the charged atmosphere. John called the party to order. He wished to propose a toast to the Great and Impressive Russian Empire (said John expansively), and to improving relations between our countries. The Russian national anthem was played through loudspeakers. John stood, one hand across his chest and the other lifting his bearskin hat. The Russians sang, and John sang in Russian. The glasses of vodka were tossed back. *Nazdarovya*, and again, and again. The waiters circulated with impressively cold trays of vodka. The Russians were delighted.

The girls – and lots of lovely locals had also poured in – suddenly found themselves far more attractive than they had ever thought – in fact they were wildly popular. Invitations were issued to leave immediately for Siberia and, once there, to spend long winters of unceasing passion. After the party, of course! Being the purveyor of the meal, I was offered several propositions, and I must admit they were tempting. These Russians left us females in no doubt that if they courted you, they really courted you. These were men who would shower you with gifts. You were informed of their intentions, which were strictly dishonourable, and they paid the most flourishing compliments. Sitting next to a hot-blooded Russian with shoulders muscled by the army, you knew that if you were in any kind of trouble there might be few survivors, but you, of course, beautiful creature that you were, would be among them. To South African women, who are used to opening their own car doors, driving home alone in the dark and much else, Russian men are a joy.

I announced lunch. Everyone was seated round the table. John was such a perceptive host: the plainer men had been seated next to the most lovely girls. They sat taller because they had been paid a compliment. There were exaggerated comments about the food. I had cooked for thirty instead of twenty-four. It was all devoured.

I was seated next to Nikolai Sobolov, who had intense blue eyes. His father had been the first to discover diamonds in Russia. I asked him if his father had become wealthy. No, not at all, it was all state property. 'Well,' I asked, 'what, if any, benefit was there to being enterprising, educated, inventive or to working hard?' His reply shattered the brilliant summer day around me. The cold face of Russia intruded.

'Our family will never be bothered by the Secret Police. We can move freely around the country. We do not need special permits.

We also are able to get more food.' Of course, the photographs at Pick 'n Pay! Who else but people who had suffered hunger would do such a thing?

John had kept the vodka supply up to industrial strength. The trays circulated constantly. It was the national anthem which finally engendered a revolt. 'Gwen, could you tell the host that we do not stand up and sing every time we have a vodka. If we did, we would not have time to get drunk!' The message was passed, and things quietened down. The Russians, who had drunk more than anyone, were perfectly sober. The South African contingent was flagging a little.

One of the men suggested to the girls that they should go swimming. They had stripped down to bikinis, which was provocative action among men like these. Two Russians, one on each side of a bikini-clad maiden, picked up the chair in which she sat, and dropped it and her into the swimming pool. Within seconds three more chairs of protesting girls followed.

Two of the Russians stood on either side of me. 'Don't even dream about it,' I said. 'I am the cook, you haven't had your last course, and if I am soaking wet I am going home.'

Someone else was chosen and dumped into the pool.

A Venetian ambassador to Muscovy, as it was called at the time in 1476, had this to say of Russians: 'Both the women and the men are handsome, but they are a brutish race. They boast of being great drunkards, and despise those who are not. The sovereign will not grant permission for everyone to make vodka, for if he did, they would be constantly intoxicated, and would murder each other like brutes.' How it has changed!

The balalaika players appeared once more. Their cheeks were pinker than I remembered on arriving. These beautiful, unselfconscious Russian men stood up and sang. They had marvellous voices, steeped in musicality. Baritones and tenors harmonised. They stood hand to heart singing songs of longing, for love and for landscape which one knew was vast, forested and snow-covered.

We were with them, sable and fox rugs pulled up to our chins. Dashing their troikas across the great snow-covered plains, forests on each side, the horses, bells jangling, were galloping to be home before nightfall. We arrived at the country dacha. Perhaps Tolstoy was there in person. Doors were flung open, we were welcomed with arms wide open, smiles, kisses, into the great heart of Russia. It was a most memorable afternoon!

Since we had a lunch party the following day, Bill and I crept away, careful to cause no disturbance. It was quieter at home. Bill wanted to look at his CDs to see exactly what they had been singing. Perhaps an hour later, we heard a car coming up the drive. I looked out of the library window. It was the Russian contingent. 'We have had the best afternoon ever. John had to go out, and he told us where to find you, so here we are.'

I opened my arms wide. There were smiles, hugs and kisses. Bottles were opened, but wine it was – we had not laid in supplies of vodka. When the visitors saw Bill's collection of CDs, they almost died of joy. Three thousand, did you say, Bill? Who can we choose first? Prokofiev, Mussorgsky, Tchaikovsky, Borodin, Shostakovich, aaahh! They were like children in a toy shop. The music was put on, and yet again they all sang. It was a private concert of startlingly good voices. Oh, how lovely it was.

Food was clearly needed, it was now eight o'clock. Our numbers were down to nine. Olive bread was defrosted. Tomorrow's cheese was put on plates. There was a country paté and hard-boiled eggs with green olive sauce, almonds and walnuts, chocolates.

They told more of their families' history, the times under Stalin – the conscriptions, the details of family life, with hardship and constant fear. It was an immense unfolding story of an enduring people. They left finally at midnight. I was devastated to see them go.

27

❧❀❧

New Year's Eve Party

I had two sons in residence. We all had been invited to a large dinner on the outskirts of the village. We checked each other out as to suitability of garb, hair and so on. 'You will do, Ma,' they said. I wasn't sure if I could say the same about them, as New Year seemed to have been well toasted from lunchtime or earlier.

Off we went. The dinner was convivial, there were old friends to greet, and talk was of fruit prices, what the Co-op was paying for export peaches, how the harvest was going, did you have mildew on the wine grapes, were there enough tourists spending their money in our dear little village? Visitors brought us news of New York, the English countryside, trips to Bangkok, what it had been like in Italy this year. Midnight arrived. Gracious! New Year

197

already, with all the potential for doing and making the same mistakes as the year before. What fun!

Everyone kissed everyone else with varying degrees of enthusiasm. We decided to join a rather raffish crowd at the local bar with garden attached. Everyone was there, young and old, landowners, visitors, drinkers, non-drinkers, farmers, tycoons, pensioners, grandmothers, children, babies, dogs, and even a parrot. The parrot's owner thought that he would be lonely at home by himself, and that he would learn some new words in the bar. The bird sat in his cage at one end of the bar, between bottles of Scotch, vodka, brandy, moonshine, tequila and other lethal beverages, testing his vocabulary. 'Happy birthday to you' was a favourite. 'Aahrn't you a pretty girl then?' he said gushingly. 'I'd like to …' I felt sure that before the evening was out, he would be able to complete the sentence.

Several of the younger women were doing their stuff on top of the bar, with the usual cat-calling from the assembly. Egged on with either 'Higher' to kick up their legs or 'Lower' to pull down their necklines, they were doing a dance routine that appeared not to have been practised. 'Turn around now, dammit' was the phrase most often used.

I danced with all kinds of people I had never seen before, and some who were familiar. It was hard to tell who was who, as the lights were switched off. Assignations were being made in drunken rapture that would not be remembered the next morning. Some spouses seemed to be looking for their 'better halves', or 'better three-quarters' in the case of one slender lady with a rather large husband. She walked crookedly, and wore only one shoe. In the garden, several random entanglements seemed to be at the point of consummation. All in all, people were finding it a jolly good party.

I thought 3 a.m. was a suitable time to leave, so I slid out of the door and went home. Saying 'Goodnight' to everyone would have taken another half an hour. I was tired and glad to crawl into bed. I was woken by the sounds of voices in the house. I lay a while hoping they would stop, but not a chance of that. Putting on a gown I went downstairs. Whoever it was, was in the kitchen having breakfast. It was 4.30 a.m.

My middle son was leaning against the kitchen counter, out of necessity. A coloured man that I had never seen before was sitting on a chair, and he was not taking chances with the forces of gravity either. He was also having a serious fluid loss, from the usual orifices.

The fridge door stood wide open. Four loaves from my precious stock of Lupo's olive bread, imported from Johannesburg, were lying on the kitchen counter, each one with a bite out of it. It was more sought after than gold, the best olive bread this side of Naples. I was indignant.

'What exactly are you doing?' I asked, 'And who is our visitor?'

'This is my bess, bess friend,' my son said, by way of introduction, 'and why is there never anything to eat in this house?'

'You seem to have made a start on things to eat, but why did you take a *hap* out of four loaves of bread?' I snarled.

'Well, every one I bit into was frozen,' he explained. 'What else is there? I'm hungry.'

'When you take something out of a freezer it's usually frozen – what did you expect? You are also very drunk, and so is your new best friend. I think his family might be missing him, so I suggest that you see him down to the road, find your way back, get into bed, and stay there.' I was not feeling hospitable or reasonable. 'And don't dare wake me before lunchtime.' I went back upstairs to bed. Quiet descended.

I was woken out of a delightful dream with the bedroom door flying open and a voice yelling, 'Where the fuck is my bakkie?' It was my youngest son. I looked at my watch. It was 5.45 a.m. 'My brother has gone off in my bakkie, and I will kill him for sure – he is too drunk to drive.'

It's no use trying to argue with someone who has clearly imbibed a good part of the Boland's wine output, all in the previous evening. 'Your brother is sleeping in the bedroom downstairs. Your truck must be on our drive.'

'That's the point, Ma. It's gone, and twenty cases of red wine on the back of it, and that's also gone.'

I thought about this. Franschhoek was known for its celebrations, but it was highly unlikely that the hotel or bottle store had reopened for business after 3 a.m. The pubs and restaurants would never have been so short-sighted as to run out of booze. I opted for clarification. 'Why don't we start at the beginning. After I left, what happened then?'

'Well, you see, a whole mob of people arrived from Paarl, and the red wine was low. Those old men, you know, husbands over fifty, they were all drinking wine and nothing else. I told them to stick to red wine, like that French doctor said, and they drank it all. Then my brother from Johannesburg, he starts to say this is a really *kak dorp* because we don't even have red wine to drink. I have the keys to the cellar, so I fetched some more wine. Do we want Franschhoek to be talked about, that it can't even give a chap a drink when he comes to a party? After that, he said he was going home, and he was too drunk to walk, so I gave him the keys to the bakkie.'

Drunken logic! 'Diffie, where are you on nights like these?' I mentally asked. Diffie was the police sergeant, usually most able in emergencies. He would have locked away a goodly portion of the population until they sobered up.

'Get dressed, Ma, we've got to find all that wine and my bakkie.' Any visions of still staying in bed were gone. I got dressed and we went out to my car. We drove in silence down the dirt road, noting several collapsed bodies on the way home from the night's festivities. Absolutely nobody was around – well, nobody who was upright, awake and capable of saying 'Good morning'.

Just as the beginnings of Le Quartier Français came in sight, I had to keep to the left. There was a vehicle parked across the white line, facing the Monument. We were within thirty metres of the police station.

'Stop, Ma,' he yelled. 'That's my bakkie! That bloody fool of a brother has left it here in the middle of the road. Oh, thank you, God, the wine is still there. Thank you, God!' All the wine was on the back of the bakkie, unmolested – twenty cases of Dion's finest. Amen!

Wine is mentioned almost instantly in the Bible. Genesis 9:20 tells us, 'Noah began to be an husbandman, and he planted a vineyard.' Unfortunately, by verse 21 'he drank of the wine, and was drunken.' But then, poor chap, he had been through rough times, building the Ark and getting all those animals sorted out. I am inclined to think that the Heavenly Father has a far less prejudiced view of wine than the bearers of his message. On this particular evening he was saving some fools from worse indiscretions.

The keys were in the ignition, the engine still on, though stalled. The entire population of Franschhoek were still in bed, if they had got that far. Nothing stirred. Thank goodness! Clearly at some point the brother from Joeys had taken his foot off the accelerator and assumed he had run out of petrol. Abandoning the bakkie, he had floundered along to the house, picking up the guest on the way.

'Tell me,' I asked, 'which way did you walk home? Or did you get a lift?'

'Ma, how else would I come home? I walk straight down this road, turn right at the Monument, walk up our dirt road, and then up to the house.' He trailed off looking puzzled, then grinned. 'Don't say it, Ma, please don't say it. I walked right past my own bakkie without seeing it, that's what I did.' Yes, boy, just like that!

'Right, now get out, take the wine back, get into your bed as soon as possible, and I don't want to see or speak to you until supper.' I waited until he had turned the bakkie in the direction of the winery, headed for home, and finally pulled the covers over my head.

Seven hours of uninterrupted sleep put a new perspective on things. We were quite pleased to see each other, retold our separate adventures, and enjoyed our supper. It was:

Olive bread and *Niçoise tapenade*
Spinach and Brie tartlets
Fresh trout, from John at Three Streams, grilled in a
salt casing
Tiny sorrel and rocket leaves, arugula and basil, all
bathed
in olive oil, lemon and walnut dressing
Balsamic fried baby tomatoes
Sformato, a fabulous Neopolitan orange cake
We did not drink any wine with the meal, but with the cake came
a *regmaker* – a splendid port from Overgaauw. Amen, amen.

28

Franschhoek Funeral

An old man, Jan, had died on the farm. He had worked for the Von Arnims, and before them for the Hugo family, as his father and Oupa had before him. He, in the Valley style, had spent his life on the tot system. On these other farms, the tot had been extended for the much older men to lunch breaks. The wine allowance was two two-pound Koo apricot jam tins full at lunchtime, and after work one or two litres of red. Ag, *but this new wine was so lekker, you could fall into temptation.* Nourished on champagne from grape juice to celestial bubbles, Ou Jan ceased to eat altogether. In a state of beatific intoxication he breathed his last.

Jan's widow, a vexatious woman whose voice was said to curdle milk, came to the manager's office to discuss the funeral arrangements. It was a Tuesday morning. On the farms which had been owned by the same families for generations, a burial plot was set aside for the owner's family, and another for the labourers' families. The widow asked if the tradition was still in place, and if Ou Jan could be put there, because Oupa en Ouma, Tante Minnie en Klein Jan were all there already. He would be lonely over in Groendal. *Wat 'n skande* if he was to be alone! It was agreed, and all went away satisfied.

It had been raining for months. The vines were pruned, the vineyards were cleared, and the new vines all planted. There was a small hiatus, in time for the grave to be dug. Four or six men volunteered to do the job. It was far better than sitting at home listening to women *tjank* and making demands on your time. *God*, they can get on a man's *senuwees*, always asking one to do this and that. *Is 'n vroumens nooit klaar nie?*

Shovels and forks were put into wheelbarrows, plus an unfortunate number of bottles of this and that, and some pegs and string to mark out the grave. The party walked off to the site, which was over a small but steep hill on a far corner of the farm near the Berg River. Hours later the diggers returned. All things considered, a very nice grave was waiting for Jan.

The stage was set. Funerals in isolated communities are a great social event. Religious ritual demands respect for the dead, if not the living. It is a time for family and friends to demonstrate solidarity. Naturally, it was obligatory to show appreciation for the guests' attendance, many of whom had come from afar.

But the weather! The rain came down in torrents for the next two days, accompanied by sleet. Almighty! *In sulke kak weer*, tea and coffee *doen niks*. It would not be wise to risk a man's health to pneumonia, *griep en hoes* when protection was so readily at hand. The guests were armed to the teeth with brandy and other pure spirits and rough reds, as white wine was believed to be for nursing mothers. These supplies were further beefed up by frequent trips to the off-sales, whose benign proprietor threw in a case of this and that to guarantee ongoing customer relations. Some of the 'this and that' should have been accompanied by a blaster's licence. It was lethal.

It was fiercely cold and also muddy. It was four o'clock, Friday afternoon. The mourners were assembled in the yard. Their clothing was motley. They were trying to shelter from the rain but it was a losing battle. There were old army overcoats from their Oupas in the Cape Corps. An ancient Desert Campaign helmet was worn by a grey-haired man of eighty who looked like a disgruntled survivor of a long-forgotten battle; he may well have looked on Rommel's forces approaching across the Egyptian desert as the Cape Corps served alongside the white troops in that campaign, with great distinction. Layers of cardigans, sweaters and scarves kept the women faintly warm. There were many capes made from black or green plastic bags. Seen collectively from a distance, they looked like a mottled caterpillar.

The Dominee had read a little prayer on not misleading the innocent; he did, after all, know his flock. The tractor was started up, and Dominee, now suitably sombre, took his place on the trailer, where lay the pathetically small pine coffin, nice and shiny with a new layer of varnish. The crowd stood mutely respectful.

The tractor started out of the yard, down the farm road, the crowd following, eyes lowered. All went according to plan until the start of the first incline. The tractor changed gear, but wheels could get no grip in mud a foot deep. The crowd, fifty strong, seemed to be slowly infected by some strange gravitational anomaly. Knees buckled, feet seemed incapable of both going in the same direction, bodies lurched, heads hung. Traction did not follow intention.

The Dominee, a practical man, got one foot firmly on top of the coffin, which was threatening to slip away off the side and into the mud. The other hand, groping under the driver's jacket, took firm hold on his belt.

'Los my uit, jou fokken moffie,' yells the driver, Gabriel, a thick-set man with a big tummy and glasses which are completely wet by the rain. When he looks around to see who the culprit is, he takes both hands off the steering wheel. 'O Jirre, Vader, o my God, I thought it was again Thomas, who is always doing like that.' Then Gabriel is yelling, 'Sit 'n klip agter, julle donners,' as the tractor now slides steadily backwards. One of the crowd, a God-fearing man, says, 'Jy, Gabriel, jy is 'n poes! You needs a windscreen wiper op jou brille. Dominee is nie 'n pansy.'

Dominee loses his grip on the coffin, which slides off the tractor into the mud. There is a delayed thud from the inside. 'O, my liewe man, hy wil uit!' screeches the widow. She has to be forcibly restrained from claiming a resurrection. The coffin reloaded on the tractor upside down has the widow screeching again. They all wait and it is set right side up, with the family now yelling about 'disrespek vir die dood'. Dominee calls everyone to order and is now firmly hanging on to the driver, and with his foot on the coffin they start up the hill once more.

The mourners were now showing a distinct lack of enthusiasm for plodding up the muddy hill. Refreshments slipped out of jacket pockets. The odd bottle of solace was shared among friends. Snot and tears, *dronkverdriet*, manifested themselves, mutterings were heard, shoves were exchanged, and fists were bunched. For some odd reason, no progress was being made. People realised that as they took one step forward and tried to follow it with the next foot, the first had slid backwards in the mud and was now down where it had started. Most of them were, in fact, giving a fair imitation of marching – no, that sounds too athletic at this juncture – of walking on the spot.

The Dominee looked around, calculated the damage, and made a plan. He told a tall man to hold on to the rear-view mirror, then someone was to hang on to him, then one by one the flock were told to hang on to each other, and a ragged human chain was formed. They held on to sleeves, shoulders, belts, jackets and hands. Unseemly groping was discouraged, and finally it could be said that they were slowly making their way up the hill.

At the top of the hill another problem had to be negotiated: how to stop sliding down the other side towards the Berg River. 'Miskien donner almal in die rivier in,' someone was heard to say. Gravity did its bit. With the brakes on, and the crowd still clustered, they slid gently downwards towards the freshly dug grave.

'Maar dis 'n fokken groot gat,' observed one of the elders. It was. 'En dis vol water.' It was too.

Anyone digging the smallest hole in the Valley between June and October will know the experience. The water table climbs to maximum and the underlying clays allow no drainage. The diggers had had no desire to go back to work or their women, the champagne had altered dimensions and perceptions, and time was of no consequence. So they had dug and drunk, and dug and drunk. The hole, now filled to overflowing, could have accommodated twenty splashing children training for the school gala.

The mourners shuffled around the grave, and there were further murmurings of unrest. The Dominee cleared his throat. His eulogy was most dignified. It was the last thing that was so. The widow began sniffing and howling. It was time to bury the dead. The pallbearers faced the problem that there was nothing to lower the coffin into, so it would have to be launched. The Dominee assisted by pushing it out with his foot. The mourners lowered their heads for prayer. They opened their eyes, and there was the coffin still floating.

Suggestions were made to put a flag on it. The Dominee prayed again, longer this time, with a mention of those lost at sea, but the coffin was still bobbing on the surface. What was to be done?

Out of the ranks stepped a nephew, a robust fisherman of sardines, yessir. He had a practical turn of mind. 'Nou kyk, almal, ek weet wat om te doen. Ons vat hom uit sy boks, en sit hom binne twee groot Pick 'n Pay sakkies, dan sit ons 'n stuk ketting rondom en ons gooi hom overboard. That is how we do it on the fishing boats when someone dies.'

The widow went berserk. 'Niemand, maar niemand, nie eers die illegitimate kind van haar skoonsuster, die hoer who can't keep her broeks up' – she paused for breath; the sister-in-law, blowsily attractive even though overweight, looked rather pleased with this unsolicited testimonial – was going to put her blameless, God-fearing husband into a supermarket bag. 'Het julle ooit so iets gehoor?' she appealed to the flagging supporters.

This signalled the crowd to split down the family fault-lines. Insults were exchanged; some mourners lost their footing and remained sitting down. But the nephew was not finished. 'No, Auntie,' he continued, 'ons sit hom net in 'n paar vuilissakkies.' He wasn't able to finish his sentence. All control was set aside and a reckless punch-up ensued. Others gave in to gravity and lay down while the coffin sailed on.

Finally the Dominee, who had had to take shelter on the tractor, called a halt. Not too soon, because up there he could referee the proceedings. It was declared a draw just as Koos aimed a low kick. Inspiration had struck the Dominee. Those members capable of standing upright were divided into two teams. Buckets and spades were located and brought on site. The bucketeers bailed, and the shovellers shovelled the surrounding mud back into the hole. The hole grew smaller and drier, and finally Ou Jan was underground. The mourners went back home and had such a jolly and drunken celebration, it was rated the best funeral for years and years.

The widow, looking rested, more robust and rosy, remarried two months later, to a man she had knocked out cold at the side of the grave. It was dark, after all, and she couldn't see that he was still at his age *fris gebou*, had his own teeth, and wore a good suit. Also, he had a clean handkerchief in his top pocket. He really had class, and was someone she had been looking for all her life; not at all like the *dronkie* she had been married to. It was really his time to go, and he went, not a day too soon for her.

The newly bespoken one had come to pay his respects three days after the funeral. It was still custom in the country for friends and family to sit with the bereaved, to be company for them, drink tea, and retell the old family stories. He had brought as gifts a bottle of cologne, a pretty sun-bonnet for the coming spring, a leg of lamb for other hungers, and his heart carried in his hand. There were also the words he had memorised, which he recited to her with all the poetry of his yearning and lonely old heart, where he still felt it was possible to welcome other springs and summers. She was so overcome, she asked him if he really meant what he said. 'I have never told a woman anything that I did not mean,' he said, looking into her face with soft brown eyes full of longing.

It took a long time for her to accept him, she told her children – altogether five minutes. She assumed the condition of a woman who was loved, from that moment. They were both old, and they decided with great confidence to 'jump straight into love'. There was no time to waste. She said she chose him because of his kisses and caresses, which were as sweet as honey, such as she hadn't had for forty years. He said he chose her because a woman who could look after herself in a difficult and emotional situation, 'and all in the dark', could surely look after him into his old age. They made a most admirable couple, doing their shopping in the village, and negotiating public disapproval at their sudden desire to be together with calm serenity and total lack of interest.

ENVOI

Leaving Franschhoek

There were reasons that I was leaving, but they are no longer important. I had made a decision, and the process was unfolding. It came down finally to an evening when I walked down to the bottom field of the farmland that was no longer mine, in the bright light of a full moon. The memory of that evening remains with me – the comfort and shelter of the trees, and the moonlight shining on the blooms of white roses.

The guinea fowl, which crossed the land above the dam each evening, were perched in the trees further down the road, clucking softly. Disorientated by the moon's brightness, the last birds were flying home above my head. A single bird, its throat banded in gold, flew close to me and flapped its wings in the humid air with a sound like fabric ripping. We seemed to have startled each other. The bird's lonely cry was like an answer to the hollow self I was at that moment.

I understood then that my years in Franschhoek were no longer than the beat of that bird's wing in the pattern of time. It was a sobering thought. I walked towards the far side of the darkness, uncertain, afraid, feeling that I was a spectre, that no search would ever be made for me, and that I was already given up for lost. Night fell down from the sky, and I stumbled towards my future.

Life was different in the city. I moved to Constantia and walked the dogs on Table Mountain three days a week. There was a high path in the pine forest where I stopped to look towards the hinterland. On clear days, I could see the outline of the Simonsberg, and I knew that behind it and a little to the east was the Valley and the home I had loved. My inner map was visual, and governed by the seasons. I stood on the path, recalling the plum trees bursting into blossom, later the fruit swelling and ripening, and the pickers cheerfully scurrying along the rows to gather it in. I saw the winter storms softening the outlines of the quiet and folded hills, the Valley cocooned and waiting for its annual resurrection. I knew, too, that these pictures were only dreams, thoughts of going back were illusions, and there was no hope of these dreams being fulfilled.

I called to the dogs, and we walked briskly back home.